浙江省普通高校"十三五"新形态教材

21世纪职业教育规划教材·旅游系列

导游英语情景口语（第三版）

主　编　陈　欣
副主编　方义桂　李文星

内 容 简 介

本书是针对应用型本科和高职高专院校培养涉外导游应用型人才而编写的教材。本着"以就业为导向,以能力为本位"的人才培养目标,其教学模式突出职业能力的训练与养成。本书打破以知识传授为主体的传统学科课程模式,采用项目、模块编排方式,以导游工作任务为核心,同时突出"情景模拟",注重听说能力的训练,让学生在模仿实践中通过完成具体项目来构建相关理论知识框架,并发展职业能力。

本书所有模块均配有由外籍专业人士朗读的录音内容,部分模块配有由导游专业教师讲解的微课视频;如任课老师需要配套教学课件,可与出版社联系索取。

图书在版编目(CIP)数据

导游英语情景口语/陈欣主编. —3版. —北京:北京大学出版社,2024.7
21世纪职业教育规划教材.旅游系列
ISBN 978-7-301-33087-6

Ⅰ.①导…　Ⅱ.①陈…　Ⅲ.①导游－英语－口语－高等职业教育－教材　Ⅳ.①F590.633

中国版本图书馆CIP数据核字(2022)第096206号

书　　　名	导游英语情景口语(第三版) DAOYOU YINGYU QINGJING KOUYU(DI-SAN BAN)
著作责任者	陈　欣　主编
责 任 编 辑	李　玥
标 准 书 号	ISBN 978-7-301-33087-6
出 版 发 行	北京大学出版社
地　　　址	北京市海淀区成府路205号　100871
网　　　址	http://www.pup.cn　　新浪微博:@北京大学出版社
电 子 邮 箱	编辑部 zyjy@pup.cn　　总编室 zpup@pup.cn
电　　　话	邮购部010-62752015　发行部010-62750672　编辑部010-62704142
印 刷 者	北京溢漾印刷有限公司
经 销 者	新华书店
	787毫米×1092毫米　16开本　19.5印张　624千字 2009年2月第1版　2012年7月第2版 2024年7月第3版　2025年1月第2次印刷　总第21次印刷
定　　　价	59.00元

未经许可,不得以任何方式复制或抄袭本书之部分或全部内容。
版权所有,侵权必究
举报电话:010-62752024　电子邮箱:fd@pup.cn
图书如有印装质量问题,请与出版部联系,电话:010-62756370

前　　言

　　《导游英语情景口语》是针对高等职业技术学院培养涉外导游应用型人才而编写的教材。高职类院校人才培养的定位是"以就业为导向，以能力为本位"，因此，其教学模式是突出职业能力的训练与养成。但是，针对涉外导游人才实践能力训练的教材在国内并不多见。为了满足实际教学的需要，我们精心编写了本书，供大家选用。

　　本书将力图打破以知识传授为主要特征的传统学科课程模式，将教学重心转变为以工作任务为核心的项目课程模式，让学生通过完成具体项目来构建相关理论知识框架，并发展职业能力。在结构设计上较传统教材有了一个创新性的改革，采用了项目、模块编排方式，强调了教材的职业性、实用性和趣味性。

　　本书具有如下几个特点：

　　1．项目、模块与任务相结合：在每一个项目（Item）下有若干个模块（Model），每个模块下设有要求学生完成的任务（Task）。

　　2．以导游实际工作程序为全书的编写体系：学生学完整本书后能够熟知导游工作流程且基本胜任涉外导游的工作。

　　3．突出听和说：每一个模块下都配有听说练习。

　　4．突出情景模拟：每一个模块下都有具体的情景实践模拟，并且给出具体步骤，方便学生学习掌握。

　　5．强调任务为核心：每一个模块都有具体的任务，引导学生循序渐进地学习。

　　全书共设有16个项目，内容涵盖了从接机到送机的涉外导游服务工作的全过程。其中，大部分项目由"3+1"个模块构成，前3个模块是根据涉外导游工作程序展开，第4个模块则是补充材料，有景点解说词、导游工作常识等。每个模块则包括以下几个任务：

　　Task 1：热身练习（Warm-up）——形式多样，有相关主题讨论、词义猜想、景点翻译等。

　　Task 2：常用词汇和句型学习（Learning Points）——所列的词汇和句型均是一线涉外导游工作中使用最频繁的，非常具有典型性。与传统涉外导游教材不同的是，本书将相关对话或者文章的生词和句型提上来，旨在让学生在学习对话或者文章前就将生词和常用句型熟记于心。

Task 3：旅游情景会话（Dialogue）——内容涉及涉外导游服务的工作程序，具有较强的实用性和可操作性。

Task 4：听力练习（Listen and Answer）——根据上面的对话内容提 5 个问题，但是要求学生通过听录音将问题写出来并回答，以锻炼其听说能力。

Task 5：角色演练（Role-play）——根据相关主题设置导游实际工作场景，要求学生根据情景操练。其中，Situation A 有具体的条目，方便学生练习；Situation B 和 Situation C 则是拓展练习。

当前，"互联网+"教育深入人心，很多院校采用线上线下混合式教学，利用信息技术创新教材形态，使新形态教材助力于课堂教学。在此背景下，本书在上一版的基础上，融入了党的"二十大"精神，同时结合"互联网+"技术，在教材形态上做了较大创新：所有模块都嵌入了音频二维码，书中带有 🔊 标志的部分都可听到由外籍专业人士朗读的录音内容，语音纯正，情景性强，便于读者模仿；部分模块还嵌入了微课视频二维码，这些视频均由导游专业教师讲解，并且模拟了英语导游真实的工作场景。如任课老师需要配套教学课件，可与出版社联系索取。

本书可供应用型本科和高职高专院校的旅游专业学生使用，也可供旅游英语爱好者自学；同时，还可作为旅游从业人员的培训材料。

本书编写分工如下：陈欣负责项目 1、2、5、6、10、12、16，李文星负责项目 3、4，方义桂负责项目 7、8、9，许文婧负责项目 11、15，滕汉华负责项目 13、14。其中，陈欣担任本书主编，并拟定编写大纲和负责统稿、修订；方义桂和李文星担任副主编。

本书在编写过程中，得到了同行业朋友们的热忱支持，还参阅了大量相关资料，在此表示衷心的感谢！尽管我们在《导游英语情景口语》的特色建设方面做出了很多的努力，但由于能力和水平有限，不当之处还望读者指正。

陈　欣
2024 年 3 月

本教材配有教学课件或其他相关教学资源，如有老师需要，可扫描右边的二维码关注北京大学出版社微信公众号"未名创新大学堂"（zyjy-pku）索取。

· 课件申请
· 样书申请
· 教学服务
· 编读往来

Contents

Item 1　Meeting Guests　迎接客人 ·· 1
　Model 1　Meeting Guests at the Airport　接机服务 ····················· 2
　Model 2　A Welcome Speech　欢迎词 ······································· 6
　Model 3　On the Way to the Hotel　至饭店途中 ·························· 9
　Model 4　China—a Country with an Ancient Civilization　中国——文明古国 ········· 14

Item 2　Hotel Check-in　饭店入住登记 ···································· 19
　Model 1　Hotel Room Reservation　预订客房 ····························· 20
　Model 2　Checking in　入住登记 ·· 24
　Model 3　Itinerary Planning　行程安排 ····································· 28
　Model 4　Process of Hotel Guest Registration　基本入住登记程序 ······· 33

Item 3　Housekeeping Service　客房服务 ································· 37
　Model 1　Escorting the Guest into the Guest Room　陪送客人进房 ······ 38
　Model 2　Making up the Room　收拾房间 ································· 42
　Model 3　About Room Service Order　客房用餐服务 ···················· 46
　Model 4　Hotels Today　今日酒店 ·· 50

Item 4　Food & Beverage Service　餐饮服务 ···························· 55
　Model 1　Reserving a Table　预订餐桌 ····································· 56
　Model 2　Food & Beverage Service　餐饮服务 ···························· 60
　Model 3　The Payment　付款 ·· 65
　Model 4　The Chinese Food　中国饮食 ····································· 69

Item 5　City Sightseeing and Transportation　都市观光和交通 ········ 75
　Model 1　City Tours　都市游 ·· 76
　Model 2　Car Rental Service　租车服务 ···································· 80
　Model 3　Xikou　溪口 ·· 85

Item 6		The Service of Travel Destinations 旅游目的地服务	91
	Model 1	Narrations on Tour 沿途讲解	92
	Model 2	At the Ticket Box 在售票处	96
	Model 3	Asking the Way 问路	100
	Model 4	The Role of a Tour Guide 导游的职责	103

Item 7		Tour of Gardens 园林游览	107
	Model 1	A Trip to the Yuyuan Garden 游览豫园	108
	Model 2	Touring the Summer Palace 游览颐和园	113
	Model 3	The Four Elements in a Traditional Garden 园林四要素	118
	Model 4	Suzhou Gardens 苏州园林	123

Item 8		Tour of Mountains 山、水之旅	129
	Model 1	In Huangshan 黄山之旅	130
	Model 2	A Trip in Guilin 游览桂林	135
	Model 3	Huangguoshu Waterfall 黄果树瀑布	140
	Model 4	West Lake 西湖	143

Item 9		Tour of Temples 中国庙宇	149
	Model 1	Visiting the Jade Buddha Temple 游览玉佛寺	150
	Model 2	Visiting the Confucius Temple 游览孔子庙	155
	Model 3	Visiting the Wudang Mountain 游览武当山	160

Item 10		Tours of Historical Sites 名胜古迹之旅	165
	Model 1	A Tour of the Forbidden City 游览紫禁城	166
	Model 2	The Tour of the Great Wall 长城之旅	170
	Model 3	The Tianyi Pavilion Library 天一阁藏书楼	174

Item 11		Tour of Chinese Characteristic Culture 中国特色文化之旅	179
	Model 1	Tai Chi 太极拳	180
	Model 2	Spring Festival 春节	184
	Model 3	Peking Opera 京剧	188
	Model 4	China-Home of Tea 茶乡中国	192

Item 12		Shopping 旅游购物	197
	Model 1	Chinese Calligraphy 中国书法	198
	Model 2	Antiques and Ancient Furniture 古玩家具	202
	Model 3	Shopping Service 购物服务	206
	Model 4	Jade Culture 玉器文化	211

Contents

Item 13　Handling Problems & Emergencies　处理问题与紧急情况 215
　Model 1　A Delayed Flight　航班延误 216
　Model 2　Calling the First Aid Center　打电话到急救中心 219
　Model 3　First Aid Techniques　急救技术 223

Item 14　Handling Customer Complaints　顾客投诉处理服务 227
　Model 1　Complaining about the Food　食品投诉 228
　Model 2　A Tour Guide or a Shopping Guide　导游还是导购 231
　Model 3　A Complaint Letter on Holiday Booking　旅游预订投诉信 235

Item 15　Checking Out　结账退房服务 239
　Model 1　Checking Out　退房服务 240
　Model 2　Paying by Credit Card　信用卡付账 244
　Model 3　Paying with a Traveler's Check　旅行支票付账 248
　Model 4　Checkout Service Procedures　退房结账程序 252

Item 16　Farewell, China　再见，中国 257
　Model 1　See you Again Soon　再见 258
　Model 2　Seeing Guests off at the Airport　机场送客 262
　Model 3　A Farewell Speech　欢送词 266

Appendix 1　The Eight Different Cooking Styles in China　中国八大菜系 271
Appendix 2　Listening material　听力材料 273

References　参考文献 302

Item 1

Meeting Guests 迎接客人

- **Model 1**
  Meeting Guests at the Airport 接机服务

- **Model 2**
  A Welcome Speech 欢迎词

- **Model 3**
  On the Way to the Hotel 至饭店途中

- **Model 4**
  China—a Country with an Ancient Civilization 中国——文明古国

Model 1
Meeting Guests at the Airport　接机服务

Task 1

Warm-up

Work in pairs. Learn the following words of the travel industry. Then answer the questions below.

airlines	travel agency	front office	housekeeping department
food and beverage department		scenic spots	shopping arcade

1. Think of two jobs in each sector.
2. Which of these jobs interest you the most? Why?

Task 2

Learning Points

Listen to the following *words, phrases,* and *useful expressions* and read along. Then try to memorize them.

🔊 **Words and Phrases**

lobby	n.	（机场）大厅
guide	n.	导游
Los Angeles	n.	[美]洛杉矶市
tired	adj.	累的，疲劳的
nevertheless	conj.	然而，不过
interesting	adj.	有趣的
luggage	n.	行李

Item 1 Meeting Guests

travel service	旅行社
tourist group	旅游团
I can manage	我能应付
shuttle bus	班车；机场内来往班车；穿梭巴士
parking lot	停车场

🔊 Useful Expressions

1. Excuse me, but are you Mr. Green from Los Angeles?
   请问您是来自洛杉矶的格林先生吗?
2. Welcome to China!
   欢迎您到中国来!
3. I sincerely hope that your visit will be pleasant and memorable.
   我竭诚祝福你们的旅行有趣而难忘!
4. Did you have a good trip?
   旅行愉快吗?
5. You all need a good rest first.
   你们都需要先休息一下。
6. You will have plenty of time to see all the places of interest in China.
   你们会有很多时间欣赏中国著名景点。
7. Is everyone in the group here?
   全团的人都在吗?
8. Have you got your checked luggage?
   你们都拿好托运行李了吗?
9. Shall I help you with your luggage?
   让我来帮您拿行李好吗?
10. The shuttle bus is just waiting in the parking lot.
    班车正在停车场等位。

Task 3

🔊 Dialogue I

Listen to *Dialogue I* for the first time. Then practise the dialogue by reading it aloud with your partner. Read through it at least twice, changing your role each time.

Meeting Guests at the Airport

【Scene】 *In the airport lobby, Meng Jun, a young tour guide from the Youth Travel Service,* is greeting a tourist group from the United States headed by James Green.

M: Meng Jun   J: James Green

M: **Excuse me, but are you Mr. Green from Los Angeles?**
J: Yes, I'm James Green.
M: Nice to meet you, Mr. Green. I'm Meng Jun, your local guide from the Youth Travel Service. Just call me Jun.
J: Nice to meet you, too.
M: (Meng Jun shakes hands with Mr. Green and other guests) **Welcome to China! I sincerely hope that your visit will be pleasant and memorable.**
J: We're so glad you've come to meet us at the airport, Jun.
M: **Did you have a good trip**, Mr. Green?
J: Yes, quite pleasant. But we feel a bit tired after the long flight.
M: Yes, you must. **You all need a good rest first.**
J: Nevertheless we are all excited that we've finally arrived in the country that we have been wishing to see for years.
M: **You will have plenty of time to see all the places of interest in China.**
J: Quite right.
M: How many people are there in your group?
J: A party of six.
M: **Is everyone in the group here? Have you got your checked luggage?**
J: Yes, of course.
M: Good. Can we go now? **Shall I help you with your luggage**, Mr. Green?
J: No, thanks. I can manage.
M: Please follow me, ladies and gentlemen! **The shuttle bus is just waiting in the parking lot.**
J: That's fine. Hurry up, guys!
M: This way, please.

Task 4

🔊 Listen and Answer

You will hear five questions. Listen carefully and give an appropriate answer to each of them.

(1) _____

(2) _____

Item 1 Meeting Guests

(3) _____
(4) _____
(5) _____

Task 5

Role-play

Act out the following dialogues.

【Situation A】 The local guide from China Youth Travel Service is at the airport to meet an inbound travel group from USA. Mr. Jones is the tour leader.

Local guide:
- ☆ Greets Mr. Jones and extends welcome to him.
- ☆ Asks about the flight.
- ☆ Thinks that Mr. Jones is possibly tired.
- ☆ Asks Mr. Jones if all members of his party are all here.
- ☆ Offers to help with the baggage.
- ☆ Says a bus will send them to the hotel.

Mr. Jones:
- ☆ Greets the local guide.
- ☆ Says the flight was a bit long.
- ☆ Answers that he had some sleep during the flight.
- ☆ Tells his wish for this trip.
- ☆ Tells the number of people in the group.
- ☆ Expresses thanks. Says he can take care of his baggage himself.

【Situation B】 You are a local guide from China International Travel Service. You are at the airport to meet a tour group of 50 people. The tour escort is Mr. Hu.

【Situation C】 At the railway station, the tour guide from local travel agency meets a foreign traveler.

Model 2
A Welcome Speech 欢迎词

Task 1

Warm-up

Work in pairs. If you are a guide, when you meet your guests for the first time, what will you say to them? Discuss with your partner.

Task 2

Learning Points

Listen to the following *words, phrases,* and *useful expressions* and read along. Then try to memorize them.

🔊 Words and Phrases

speech	n.	发言，演说
introduce	v.	介绍
team	n.	团队
trip	n.	旅行
driver	n.	司机
suggestion	n.	建议
hesitate	v.	犹豫
driving experience		驾龄

🔊 Useful Expressions

1. Good morning, everyone.
   大家早上好。

2. Let me introduce my team to you first.
   首先让我来向大家介绍一下我的团队。
3. I'm your tour guide.
   我是你们的导游。
4. And this is Mr. Deng, our driver, who has 10 years of driving experience.
   这是我们的司机邓师傅，他有着10年的驾龄。
5. We will do our best to make your trip more enjoyable and memorable.
   我们将尽最大努力使你们的旅行更有趣、更难忘。
6. If you have any problems or suggestions, please don't hesitate to let us know.
   如果你们有任何问题或者建议，请尽管告诉我们。
7. I hope you will have a pleasant stay in the city.
   希望你们在这个城市玩得愉快。

Task 3

🔊 Dialogue II

Listen to *Dialogue II* for the first time. Then practise the dialogue by reading it aloud with your partner. Read through it at least twice, changing your role each time.

A Welcome Speech

【Scene】 *The tour guide met the tour group at the airport and they are driving to the hotel. On the shuttle bus, the tour guide is giving a welcome speech.*

G: guide   L: leader

G: Is everybody on the bus?
L: Yes, I think so.
G: Shall we go now?
L: Yes, please.
G: OK. **Good morning, everyone.** Welcome to Ningbo. **Let me introduce my team to you first.** My name is Huang Lan. You may call me Lan. **I'm your tour guide** from the Youth Travel Service. I'll be with you for your trip in Ningbo. **And this is Mr. Deng, our driver, who has 10 years of driving experience.** We're glad to have all of you here. **We will do our best to make your trip more enjoyable and memorable. If you have any problems or suggestions, please don't hesitate to let us know. I hope you will have a pleasant stay in the city.** Thank you very much!

Task 4

🔊 Listen and Answer

You will hear five questions. Listen carefully and give an appropriate answer to each of them.

(1) _____
(2) _____
(3) _____
(4) _____
(5) _____

Task 5

Speaking

Make a "Welcome Speech" with your partner.

Item 1 Meeting Guests

Model 3
On the Way to the Hotel 至饭店途中

Task 1

Warm-up

Work in pairs. Learn the following words of the industry. Then answer the questions below.

safari park	festival	amusement park
historic building	place of natural beauty	

Which of these tourist attractions would interest you the most? Why?

Task 2

Learning Points

Listen to the following *words, phrases,* and *useful expressions* and read along. Then try to memorize them.

 Words and Phrases

conduct	v.	组织，为（某人）导游
wonderland	n.	仙境
spring	n.	泉水
waterfall	n.	瀑布
scenery	n.	风景
hometown	n.	家乡
recreation	n.	娱乐
locate	v.	位于

downtown	n.	市中心
service	n.	服务
coastal city		沿海城市
historic city		历史名城
scenic spot		景点
Tianyi Square		天一广场
The Old Bund		老外滩
Three-River Mouth		三江口
aircraft carrier		航母
The Drum Tower		鼓楼
leisure facility		休闲设施
reception desk		前台

🔊 Useful Expressions

1. I'd like to introduce something about this city.
   我想要介绍一下有关这座城市的一些情况。
2. It is a famous historic city.
   它是一座历史文化名城。
3. There're many famous scenic spots.
   这有很多著名的景点。
4. Ningbo is a wonderland of water.
   宁波是水之仙境。
5. Ningbo attracts a large number of domestic and foreign tourists every year.
   每年宁波都吸引了大批的海内外游客前来参观游览。
6. It is known as the "Business Aircraft Carrier of Ningbo" and the "Face of Ningbo City".
   它被誉为宁波的商业航母，是宁波一张亮丽的名片。
7. It is the only ancient gate tower left in Ningbo.
   它是宁波唯一的一座古城楼。
8. It is located downtown.
   它位于市中心。
9. It offers warm and efficient service.
   它提供热情有效的服务。
10. We shall meet at the hotel lobby at 7:00 a.m. for our first visit tomorrow.
    我们明天上午7点在酒店大堂集合开始首次旅行。

Task 3

🔊 **Dialogue III**

Listen to *Dialogue III* for the first time. Then practise the dialogue by reading it aloud with your partner. Read through it at least twice, changing your role each time.

On the Way to the Hotel

【Scene】*On the way to the hotel, the tour guide is conducting the first bus tour guiding.*

G: guide   L: leader   T: tourist

G: OK, everyone. Now, **I'd like to introduce something about this city.** Ningbo is a coastal city in Zhejiang Province of China. **It is a famous historic city** with rich cultural heritage. **There're many famous scenic spots,** such as Tianyi Square, the Old Bund, Tianyi Pavilion Library, Xikou Scenic Area, Dongqian Lake, and so on. **Ningbo is a wonderland of water.** There are numerous rivers, lakes, springs, waterfalls, wells, and harbors. **Ningbo attracts a large number of domestic and foreign tourists every year.**

L: We are really longing for a visit.

G: You must be tired after the long trip. I'm afraid you need a good rest first.

L: That's very kind of you.

T: Oh, look, how beautiful the scenery is!

G: Yes, it is the Three-River Mouth, in Chinese we say Sanjiangkou. It is the center of the Ningbo City.

L: What are the three rivers?

G: One is the Yuyao River. Another one is called the Fenghua River. It runs from the famous scenic spot Xikou of Fenghua, Mr. Chiang Kai-Shek's hometown. The two rivers then join with another river, the Yongjiang River. The three rivers form a "Y" shape, which makes it special. Please look, that's Tianyi Square. It is the largest "one-stop" shopping and recreation center in the country.

L: Oh, what a big square!

G: Yes, **it is known as the "Business Aircraft Carrier of Ningbo" and the "Face of Ningbo City".**

L: That's rather interesting. How many shops does it have?

G: Now the square has over 800 shops of various kinds.

T: What about that building?
G: It is the Drum Tower. **It is the only ancient gate tower left in Ningbo.**
T: I see, it looks magnificent.
L: Well, how long will it take to get to the hotel?
G: It'll take us only half an hour. **It is located downtown.**
L: Can you talk more about the hotel?
G: Yes, of course. The hotel is the Sheraton hotel. It is one of the best five-star hotels in the city. **It offers warm and efficient service.** The leisure facilities in the hotel are extensive, such as a swimming pool, sauna, health centre, bowling, beauty salon, and so on. I hope you will enjoy your stay there.
L: That's great.
G: Well, here we are. Let's get off and go to the reception desk. **We shall meet at the hotel lobby at 7:00 a.m. for our first visit tomorrow.** Please do remember the plate number of our bus. The number is 19288.
L: OK. Hurry up, guys!

Task 4

Listen and Answer

You will hear five questions. Listen carefully and give an appropriate answer to each of them.

(1) _____
(2) _____
(3) _____
(4) _____
(5) _____

Task 5

Role-play

Act out the following dialogues.

【Situation A】 You are an English tour guide who is meeting an American tour group at the airport in Hangzhou. On the way to the hotel, you are supposed:

☆ to make a welcome speech.

Item 1 Meeting Guests

☆ to brief on the city.
☆ to explain the scene along the way.
☆ to say something about the hotel.
☆ to announce the assembling time and place.

Discuss with your partner, and then present it by yourself.

【Situation B】 You, a local guide, met a tour group at the bus station in Ningbo. On the way to the hotel, you are introducing Ningbo to your tourists.

Model 4
China—a Country with an Ancient Civilization
中国——文明古国

Task 1

Learning Points

Listen to the following *words, phrases,* and *useful expressions* and read along. Then try to memorize them.

🔊 Words and Phrases

ancient	adj.	古老的，古代的
civilization	n.	文明
inventor	n.	发明者
compass	n.	指南针
printing	n.	印刷术
resource	n.	（常作复数）资源
elegant	adj.	雅致的，优美的
waterfalls	n.	瀑布
rare	adj.	稀有的，罕见的
species	n.	（常作复数）（生物）种，种类
distinctive	adj.	有特色，特别的
cuisine	n.	烹饪
domestic	adj.	家的，本国的
political	adj.	国家的，政治的
contemporary	adj.	当代的，现代的
cultural relics		文化遗迹
historical sites		名胜古迹
look forward to (doing)		期待（做）

Item 1 Meeting Guests

🔊 Useful Expressions

1. China has a written history of over 5,000 years of civilization and boasts rich cultural relics and historical sites.
   中国有着五千多年的灿烂文化和丰富的历史文化遗迹。
2. China attracts a large number of domestic and foreign tourists every year.
   中国每年都吸引着大量的国内外游客。
3. Beijing, the capital city of the People's Republic of China, is the country's political and cultural center.
   中华人民共和国的首都——北京，是国家的政治和文化中心。
4. Beijing, as well as the whole country of China, is looking forward to welcoming friends from all over the world!
   北京，以及全中国都在盼望着迎接来自世界各地的朋友们！

Task 2

🔊 Passage Reading

Listen to the short passage for the first time. Then practise it by reading it aloud by yourself.

China—a Country with an Ancient Civilization

China has a written history of over 5,000 years of civilization and boasts rich cultural relics and historical sites. It is the inventor of the compass, papermaking, gunpowder, and printing. Thanks to China's rich tourist resources ——high mountains, elegant rivers, springs, and waterfalls, rich and varied folk customs, rare species, scenic spots and historical sites, distinctive opera, music and dance, and world-famous cuisine, **China attracts a large number of domestic and foreign tourists every year.**

Beijing, the capital city of the People's Republic of China, is the country's political and cultural center. It is also one of the world's most famous historical and cultural cities where you can learn about the country's history spanning over 1,000 years.

Beijing, as well as the whole country of China, is looking forward to welcoming friends from all over the world!

Task 3

🔊 Listen and Answer

You will hear five questions. Listen carefully and give an appropriate answer to each of them.

(1) _____

(2) _____

(3) _____

(4) _____

(5) _____

Task 4

Oral Practice

Retell the text in your own words.

Task 5

More Oral and Listening Practice:

【Listening】Listen to the following dialogue and passage and fill in the blanks.

🔊 Listening I

At the Airport

    A: Zhu Lan   B: Mark Davis   C: Miss Tyler

A: _____?

B: Why, yes, I'm Mark Davis.

A: Oh, Mr. Davis. _____. My name is Zhu Lan. _____.

B: Hello, Ms Zhu. Thank you for coming to meet us.

A: Welcome to China Mr. Davis. _____?

B: Fine. We had a very pleasant flight. _____, my assistant. She is in charge of the daily affairs of our tour group.

Item 1 Meeting Guests

A: How do you do, Miss Tyler? _____.
C: How do you do? I'm pleased to meet you, too.
A: We've made reservations for your group at the Hong Kong Garden Hotel.
C: Thank you very much.
A: Shall we _____? _____ outside.
C: Fine.
A: Your _____ in the hotel.
C: That's good.
A: _____, Mr. Davis?
B: It's very kind of you.

🔊 **Listening II**

Traveling in Beijing

There are many fascinating sights in and _____ Beijing, but before visiting the attractions, _____ an hour or two walking the streets. _____ off the main boulevards and _____ through the maze-like alleys where _____ residents live or perhaps stroll down Old Culture Street. If your hotel is _____, walk to the walled 14th-century Forbidden City, so _____ because it was off limits to ordinary citizens. On its grounds are six palaces and 800 smaller buildings, containing _____ rooms. The main gate of the _____ opens onto Tian'anmen Square. The square is the _____ of the _____ to the People's Heroes, Chairman Mao Zedong Memorial Hall, the _____ of the People, the Museum of Chinese _____, and the Museum of the Chinese _____.

【Topics】 Divide the class into groups. Choose one of the following topics to discuss in each group. Give a short report about the group's opinion after that.

1. What do you think of the definition of tourism?
2. Do you think our daily lives will be greatly affected by the development of tourism? Why or why not?
3. Which is your favorite way of traveling, package tour or independent traveling? Why?

Item 2

○○○○

Hotel Check-in　饭店入住登记

- **Model 1**
  Hotel Room Reservation　预订客房

- **Model 2**
  Checking in　入住登记

- **Model 3**
  Itinerary Planning　行程安排

- **Model 4**
  Process of Hotel Guest Registration　基本入住登记程序

Model 1
Hotel Room Reservation 预订客房

Task 1

Warm-up

Work in pairs. Learn the following words of the sectors of the hotel services. Then answer the questions below.

reserve	hotel	inn	star-hotel
single	double deluxe	bath	shower

1. When you are arranging for a room reservation, what information should you include?
2. Name different types of hotels. What is the main difference among these different types of hotels?
3. Discuss the different types of rooms of a hotel.

Task 2

Learning Points

Listen to the following *words, phrases,* and *useful expressions* and read along. Then try to memorize them.

🔊 Words and Phrases

client	*n.*	顾客，客户，委托人
luxurious	*adj.*	奢侈的，豪华的
reservation	*n.*	（旅馆房间）预定
deluxe	*adj.*	豪华的，华丽的
presidential	*adj.*	总统的

confirm	v.	确认
suite	n.	（一套）家具，套房

🔊 Useful Expressions

1. This is Hu Hong, the tour guide of China Youth Travel Agency.
   我是中国青年旅行社的导游胡红。
2. I'd like to reserve a room in Guangzhou.
   我想在广州预订一个房间。
3. What kind of room would you like to reserve?
   请问您想要预订什么样的房间？
4. How long would you stay here?
   请问您要住几天？
5. There would be some discount when the hotel is not very busy.
   当酒店不太忙的时候，可以打折。
6. Is there anything else I can do for you?
   请问还有别的事吗？
7. Just call me when you have other questions.
   如果有其他问题，请呼叫我。

Task 3

🔊 Dialogue I

Listen to *Dialogue I* for the first time. Then practice the dialogue by reading it aloud with your partner. Read through it at least twice, changing your role each time.

Hotel Room Reservation

G: guide   C: client

G: **This is Hu Hong, the tour guide of China Youth Travel Agency.** Can I help you?

C: This is John Smith from London. **I'd like to reserve a room in Guangzhou.** Will you please arrange it for me?

G: It's my pleasure. **What kind of room would you like to reserve?** We have singles, doubles, suites of different styles, deluxe ones.

C: A British suite, please.

G: OK. **How long would you stay here?**
C: Three days from the third to the fifth of March.
G: Now, Mr. Smith, let's check the information. You'd like to reserve a British suite for three days from the third to the fifth of March. Is that so?
C: Yes, exactly.
G: **Is there anything else I can do for you?**
C: Can you give some idea about the price for the hotel?
G: Well, it's about 1000 RMB for one day. **And there would be some discount when the hotel is not very busy.**
C: OK. I see. Thank you for the information.
G: Thank you for calling. We look forward to seeing you. **Just call me when you have other questions.**
C: Thank you. Bye!
G: Goodbye.

Task 4

🔊 Listen and Answer

You will hear five questions. Listen carefully and give an appropriate answer to each of them.

(1) _____
(2) _____
(3) _____
(4) _____
(5) _____

Task 5

Role-play

Act out the following dialogues.

【Situation A】 Wu Fei, a tour guide of Rainbow Travel Agency is receiving the phone. Eleanor Swan is a foreign guest who wants to make a reservation through Rainbow Travel Agency. They are having a conversation about the reservation.

Guide:

☆ Upon receiving the call, greets Eleanor Swan and makes a self introduction.
☆ Offers help.
☆ Tells the different kinds of rooms and their respective prices.
☆ Asks the kind of room Eleanor Swan would like to reserve.
☆ Asks the date Eleanor Swan would like to stay.
☆ Asks to check the information.
☆ Says goodbye and express good wishes.

Client:

☆ Greets the guide and gives a self introduction.
☆ Asks to reserve a room.
☆ Asks the different prices of different rooms.
☆ Asks to reserve a double-room with a bath.
☆ Tells the date he/she would stay.
☆ Confirms the information with guide.
☆ Expresses thanks.

【Situation B】 A Chinese tour guide makes a group reservation for 28 guests to stay in New York for two days.

【Situation C】 A French travel agency asks a Chinese tour guide to reserve a room for Mr. Steve to stay in Nanjing for three days.

Model 2
Checking in　入住登记

Task 1

Warm-up

Work in pairs. Learn the following words of the travel industry. Then answer the question below.

museum	theatre	gallery	church or temple
residence of a famous person		downtown	recreational center

What place would you recommend to the tourists when you escort them to a new city? Why?

Task 2

Learning Points

Listen to the following *words, phrases,* and *useful expressions* and read along. Then try to memorize them.

🔊 Words and Phrases

Sino-German	n.	中德
delegation	n.	代表团
sea-view	n.	海景
superior	adj.	优越的
name list		名单
passport	n.	护照
voucher	n.	凭证，[美]优惠购货券

Item 2 Hotel Check-in

check in	入住登记
twin room	双人间
group visa	团体签证
room card	房卡
morning call service	叫醒服务
breakfast buffet	自助早餐
dining hall	餐厅

🔊 Useful Expressions

1. We'd like to check in.
   我们要办理登记入住。
2. Would you please tell me the name of your group?
   您可以告诉我你们团队的名称吗？
3. Here is the name list with the group visa.
   这是名单和集体签证。
4. May I take a look at your passport?
   我可以看下您的护照吗？
5. Could you please fill out this check-in form, please?
   您可以填一下这张入住登记表吗？
6. Here are the room cards.
   这些是房卡。
7. Do you need a morning call service?
   你们需要叫醒服务吗？
8. The breakfast will be served in the dining hall on the second floor.
   早餐在二楼餐厅用餐。

Task 3

🔊 Dialogue II

Listen to *Dialogue II* for the first time. Then practise the dialogue by reading it aloud with your partner. Read through it at least twice, changing your role each time.

Checking in

【Scene】 *The tour guide Meng Lan and the tour leader Sherry are helping a group of foreign visitors to check in at a hotel in Ningbo. The reception clerk receives them.*

C: clerk   G: guide   L: leader

C: Good morning, madam. May I help you?
G: Yes, please. This is the group leader, Sherry. **We'd like to check in.**
C: OK. Nice to meet you, Sherry.
L: Nice to meet you, too.
C: Do you have reservations?
G: Yes. The Ningbo Youth Travel Agency has booked 15 rooms for us.
C: **Would you please tell me the name of your group?**
L: The Sino-German Friendship Bridge Delegation.
C: A moment, please.
   (*The clerk looks up the information on the computer.*)
C: Yes, 2 deluxe sea-view rooms, 3 superior suites and 10 twin rooms for three nights.
G: Yes, exactly. **Here is the name list with the group visa.**
C: Thank you. You are well prepared. **May I take a look at your passport**, Miss Sherry?
L: Here you are. (*She hands the clerk her passport.*)
C: **Could you please fill out this check-in form, please, Miss Sherry?**
L: OK. Here you are. (*She fills out the form.*)
C: OK. **Here are the room cards. Do you need a morning call service?**
G: Yes, please set it for 7:00 a.m. tomorrow morning and 8:00 a.m. for the rest of the days.
C: Here are the vouchers for your breakfast buffet. **The breakfast will be served in the dining hall on the second floor** from 7:00 to 9:00 a.m.
G: Thank you.
L: Thank you.
C: I wish you a pleasant stay here.

Task 4

🔊 Listen and Answer

You will hear five questions. Listen carefully and give an appropriate answer to each of them.

(1) _____

(2) _____

(3) _____

(4) _____

(5) _____

Task 5

Role-play

Act out the following dialogues.

【Situation A】 An English tour guide is leading a Chinese tour group to a five-star hotel in a foreign city. He is helping the group to check in. There is a conversation between the guide and the clerk of the hotel.

Clerk:
☆ Greets the guide and offers help.
☆ Asks whether the guide has a reservation.
☆ Asks the guide to wait a moment while checking the reservation on the computer, (upon finding the reservation) confirms the reservation.
☆ Says the group should show their passports and visas.
☆ (Gives the keys to the rooms) Tells the floor and rooms.
☆ Reminds the group of security and the deposit money or other valuable things for free.
☆ Wishes the group to have a happy stay.

Tour guide:
☆ Greets the clerk and makes a self introduction.
☆ Says the group has a reservation.
☆ Confirms the reservation that they would stay in the hotel for 4 days.
☆ Collects the groups' passports and visas and gives them to the clerk.
☆ Tells the group to choose rooms by themselves, then make a list and gives it to the clerk.
☆ Thanks and relays the information to the group.
☆ Expresses thanks and says goodbye.

【Situation B】 A tour escort of a group from Canada is helping the group to check in. You are the local tour guide to receive the group. Make a conversation concerning the process of check-in. A third person can be invited to act as the clerk of the hotel.

Model 3
Itinerary Planning 行程安排

听力音频　微课视频

Task 1

Warm-up

Work in pairs. If you are a guide in Beijing, when you tell your guests the itinerary of a three-day city tour, what will you say to them? Discuss it with your partner.

Task 2

Learning Points

Listen to the following *words, phrases,* and *useful expressions* and read along. Then try to memorize them.

🔊 **Words and Phrases**

satisfy	v.	使满意
itinerary	n.	旅程
arrangement	n.	安排
seafood	n.	海鲜
taste	v.	品尝
snack	n.	小吃
advice	n.	建议
pavilion	n.	阁，亭
tourist	n.	游客
detour	n.	绕道
regulation	n.	规则
director	n.	主管
scenic area		景区

Item 2 Hotel Check-in

🔊 **Useful Expressions**

1. Have you seen the itinerary planning?
   您看旅游行程表了吗?
2. Let's check it again.
   我们再仔细核对一下。
3. The tour in Ningbo will last two days.
   这次宁波游共两天。
4. We'll have lunch at Shipu Restaurant, which is a famous seafood restaurant in Ningbo.
   午餐安排在宁波著名的海鲜酒店石浦饭店。
5. Do you have any other advice?
   您有其他建议吗?
6. It is said that the Tianyi Pavilion is very famous in Ningbo!
   听说宁波的天一阁很有名气!
7. Many tourists in the group are interested in it.
   这个团有很多客人都对它很感兴趣。
8. Can you arrange the tour for us?
   不知道能不能安排?
9. But there will be some extra cost for the detour.
   不过,要专程去(天一阁)就存在绕路的问题,可能会产生一些费用。
10. If tourists agree, we'll pay according to the regulations.
    若客人们同意,我们将按规定支付。
11. The director of our company has agreed the arrangement.
    我们公司的主管已经同意了这个安排。
12. I'll ask the tourists for advice later.
    回头我再向客人们征求一下意见。

Task 3

🔊 **Dialogue III**

Listen to *Dialogue III* for the first time. Then practise the dialogue by reading it aloud with your partner. Read through it at least twice, changing your role each time.

Itinerary Planning

G: guide   L: leader

G: Sherry, are the tourists satisfied with rooms?

L: Very good, thanks a lot. You've done a good job.

G: It's my pleasure. **Have you seen the itinerary planning?**

L: Yes, a good arrangement.

G: Thanks. **Let's check it again. The tour in Ningbo will last two days.** On the first day, we'll go to Tianyi Square first which is the biggest square in Ningbo. The tour will last three hours. **We'll have lunch at Shipu Restaurant, which is a famous seafood restaurant in Ningbo.** And then we'll go to Drum Tower. The tour will last two hours. We'll have dinner in Gangyagou Restaurant, where you can taste different kinds of snacks of Ningbo. On the second day, we'll go to Xikou of Fenghua which is the hometown of Chiang Kai-shek. We'll stay there for the whole day and finish the lunch and supper in the Xikou scenic area.

L: Quite right.

G: **Do you have any other advice?**

L: Oh, yes. **It is said that the Tianyi Pavilion is very famous in Ningbo!**

G: Yes, it is the oldest library in Asia now.

L: **Many tourists in the group are interested in it.** It will be perfect to go to visit the Tianyi Pavilion. **Can you arrange the tour for us?**

G: Of course. **But there will be some extra cost for the detour.**

L: No problem. **If tourists agree, we'll pay according to the regulations.**

(*The guide calls to the director of travel agency for advice.*)

G: **The director of our company has agreed the arrangement.** But every tourist should pay another 30 yuan for detour. Do you agree?

L: OK, thanks a lot. **I'll ask the tourists for advice later.**

G: If we go to visit the Tianyi Pavilion, it will be the first scenic spot tomorrow. But we should hurry up. Can you tell the tourists?

L: All right.

G: Please tell the tourists to bring their sunglasses, umbrella, and a hat as the weather is sunny.

L: Yes, thank you.

G: I hope all of you will enjoy the tour. See you in the morning.

L: See you.

Item 2 Hotel Check-in

Task 4

🔊 Listen and Answer

You will hear five questions. Listen carefully and give an appropriate answer to each of them.

(1) _____
(2) _____
(3) _____
(4) _____
(5) _____

Task 5

Role-play

Act out the following dialogs.

【Situation A】 Make an itinerary plan around the city Hangzhou to include Lingyin Temple and the West Lake with your partner.

Tour guide:
☆ Greets the guests.
☆ Says the next day they'll visit Lingyin Temple and the West Lake.
☆ Tells the time and place to meet.
☆ Tells the time to get to the two places respectively and how long the tour lasts.
☆ Tells the things to prepare according to the weather.
☆ Says the lunch will be taken in a snack bar.
☆ Says they would go by coach.
☆ Tells the time to return to the hotel.
☆ Thanks for attention and wishes them a nice tour.

Guest(s):
☆ Greets the guide.
☆ Agrees warmly and expresses eagerness for longing for the famous places.
☆ Asks the time and place to meet.
☆ Asks how long the tour will last.
☆ Asks what to prepare.

☆ Asks where to have lunch.
☆ Asks how they would go to the two places.
☆ Asks when they would go back to the hotel.
☆ Thanks for the information.

【**Situation B**】 Make a conversation about an itinerary plan with your partner. You can choose different cities or areas, but you should include at least two scenic spots.

Model 4
Process of Hotel Guest Registration
基本入住登记程序

Task 1

Learning Points

Listen to the following *words, phrases,* and *useful expressions* and read along. Then try to memorize them.

🔊 **Words and Phrases**

approach	v.	走近
establish	v.	确立，建立
title	n.	称呼
assign	v.	分配
deposit	n.	押金
cardholder	n.	持卡人
validity	n.	有效
receipt	n.	收据
cashier	n.	收银员
eye contact		目光接触

🔊 **Useful Expressions**

1. Greet each guest with a smile in your voice as well as on your face.
   向客人问好时不仅要面带微笑，声音里也应该透着微笑。
2. You should first establish and keep eye contact with the guest.
   你首先要和客人有目光接触。
3. When addressing the guest, do not call a guest by his or her first name.
   称呼客人，不可直呼其名。
4. Ask the guest to show his or her credit card for an imprint or to pay a deposit.
   请客人出示信用卡将其复印，或者让他交押金。

Task 2

🔊 **Passage Reading**

Listen to the short passage for the first time. Then practise it by reading it aloud by yourself.

Process of Hotel Guest Registration

If you are a reception clerk at the reception desk, you should always **greet each guest with a smile in your voice as well as on your face.** When a guest is approaching, **you should first establish and keep eye contact with the guest.** Then try to find out the guest's name immediately and use it during the conversation. Always use polite titles as "Mr." or "Ms." **When addressing the guest, do not call a guest by his or her first name.**

Next, find out if the guest has a reservation. Then, check the reservation in the computer and confirm the room information with the guest.

After that, ask the guest to show his or her passport and to fill out the registration form. When the form is ready, you should try to find out the needs of the guest, e.g. the position of the room.

Then, assign a room to the guest and prepare the key to the room. Before giving the key to the guest, **ask the guest to show his or her credit card for an imprint or to pay a deposit.** Upon receiving the credit card, check the name of the cardholder and its validity. Collect 150% of the room rate and give the guest the receipt. Next, confirm with the guest the departure date, room rate, and other needs. Fill out the room card and tell the guest the room number. If there's nothing wrong, give the guest the room card and key to the room. When everything is done, thank the guest and wish them a pleasant stay.

At last, turn in the guest registration form, credit card imprint and a copy of deposit receipt to the cashier.

Task 3

🔊 **Listen and Answer**

You will hear five questions. Listen carefully and give an appropriate answer to each of them.

(1) _____

(2) _____

(3) _____

(4) _____

(5) _____

Task 4

Oral Practice

Retell the text in your own words.

Task 5

More Oral and Listening Practice:

【Listening】 Listen to the dialogues and fill in the blanks.

Listening I

A Group Reservation

R: Receptionist   C: Customer

R: Good morning. Reservations. _____?
C: Good morning. I'd like to _____.
R: What type of rooms do you want to reserve?
C: We have 10 people. _____, please.
R: For which dates?
C: From _____ of March.
R: Wait a minute, please. _____ for March from _____.
    Yes, those rooms are _____.
C: What will be the rate?
R: It's _____ per night.
C: Can you give us _____ since we always _____ _____?
R: May I have your name, please?

C: Brutes Lewis from General Traveling Company.
R: Oh, Yes, Mr. Lewis, there is a _____ percent discount for regular customers.
C: How can I _____?
R: You can guarantee the reservation with your _____.
C: My _____ is 3600 54762 5819.
R: OK. Mr. Lewis. How will you be arriving?
C: _____. Do you have _____ service?
R: When will you be arriving at the airport?
C: The arrival time should be _____.
R: OK. Our hotel bus will be there at that time.

Listening II

Extending the Stay

R: Receptionist   G: Guest

R: Good morning, sir. _____?
G: I meant to check out today, but I have to _____.
R: May I know your _____, please?
G: Andrew Stowe of Room 618.
R: Please _____, Mr. Stowe. I'll _____. Here, today is 12th. You _____?
G: Yes, exactly.
R: I'm sorry, sir. You can only stay in that room _____. Your floor was reserved for a conference _____.
G: What will be my _____?
R: Would you mind changing to room _____?
C: Not at all.
R: Thank you, sir. This is your registration form. Please _____ _____.
G: OK.

【Topics】Divide the class into groups. Choose one of the following topics to discuss in each group. Give a short report about the group's opinion after that.

1. When you go traveling, what kind of hotel would you prefer? Why?
2. Why do you think teamwork is essential in the running of a good hotel?
3. Comment on the advantages and disadvantages of working as a hotel front desk clerk.

Item 3

☐☐☐☐

Housekeeping Service　客房服务

● **Model 1**
  Escorting the Guest into the Guest Room　陪送客人进房

● **Model 2**
  Making up the Room　收拾房间

● **Model 3**
  About Room Service Order　客房用餐服务

● **Model 4**
  Hotels Today　今日酒店

Model 1
Escorting the Guest into the Guest Room
陪送客人进房

Task 1

Warm-up

Work in pairs. Learn the following words about hotel services. Then answer the questions below.

front office	housekeeping	food preparation
F& B service	marketing	accounting

1. What sector of the hotel industry most appeals to you?
2. Think of two positions in each sector.
3. When doing housekeeping service, what should the attendant pay attention to?

Task 2

Learning Points

Listen to the following *words, phrases,* and *useful expressions* and read along. Then try to memorize them.

🔊 Words and Phrases

usher	v.	引领
spacious	adj.	宽敞的
wardrobe	n.	衣柜
faucet	n.	水龙头

Item 3 Housekeeping Service

switch	*n.*	开关
laptop	*n.*	手提电脑
lobby attendant		大堂服务员
safe-deposit box		保险箱

🔊 Useful Expressions

1. Welcome to our floor.
   欢迎光临本楼层。
2. I'm the attendant for this floor.
   我是本楼层的服务员。
3. There is a price list over there.
   那里有一个价目单。
4. There is an internet broadband access hookup on the desk.
   桌子上有一个宽带上网接口。
5. If you need any help, please let me know.
   如果您需要帮助，请告诉我。

Task 3

🔊 Dialogue I

Listen to *Dialogue I* for the first time. Then practise the dialogue by reading it aloud with your partner. Read through it at least twice, changing your role each time.

Escorting the Guest into the Guest Room

【Scene】 *The lobby attendant ushers Mr. Jones onto the floor of his room. The floor attendant, Xiao Hu is waiting for them.*

        L: Lobby attendant   X: Xiao Hu   J: Jones

L: Hello, Xiao Hu. This is Mr. Jones of Room 1506.
X: Nice to meet you, Mr. Jones. **Welcome to our floor**.
J: Nice to meet you, too.
X: **I'm the attendant for this floor**. We're glad to have you here. This way, please.
J: Good.

X: Here we are. This is your room, Mr. Jones.
J: Oh, the room seems very spacious!
X: Yes. Mr. Jones, could I put your suitcase by the wardrobe?
J: Yes, please.
X: Well, Mr. Jones, let me introduce the facilities in the room. First, let's see the bathroom. The red faucet is for hot water and the white one is for cold water.
J: Is the water drinkable?
X: No. You may get hot drinking water from the mini jar, and cold drinks from the mini bar.
J: Do you have a price list for the things in the mini bar?
X: Yes, **there is a price list over there**. Well, and this is the air conditioning switch. The temperature in your room can be adjusted as you like.
J: Can I make IDD calls in the room?
X: Yes. For IDD calls, just dial 9, and then 0-0. Next, dial the country code and the area code before the phone number you want to call. Besides, there is a phone index on the desk.
J: I see. Is the Internet available through my laptop?
X: Certainly. **There is an Internet broadband access hookup on the desk**.
J: How much do you charge for the use of it?
X: It's 5 RMB per hour. Would you please keep your valuables in the safe-deposit box in the wardrobe?
J: Certainly. Thank you so much.
X: It's my pleasure. **If you need any help, please let me know**.

Task 4

🔊 Listen and Answer

You will hear five questions. Listen carefully and give an appropriate answer to each of them.

(1) _____

(2) _____

(3) _____

(4) _____

(5) _____

Task 5

Role-play

Act out the following dialogs.

【Situation A】 The lobby attendant escorts Mr. Johnson to the floor attendant. And the floor attendant escorts Mr. Johnson into his room.

Lobby attendant:
☆ Greets Mr. Johnson.
☆ Introduces Mr. Johnson to the floor attendant

The floor attendant:
☆ Greets Mr. Johnson and extends welcome to him.
☆ Introduces the basic facilities in the room, (bathroom, water, remote control, etc.)
☆ Tells Mr. Johnson that IDD calls could be made after being activated.
☆ Tells Mr. Johnson that Internet is available and free of charge.
☆ Tells Mr. Johnson that there are room services for food and drink and that there is a price list on the desk.
☆ Tells Mr. Johnson that other help is available when being requested.

Mr. Johnson:
☆ Greets the lobby attendant.
☆ Greets the floor attendant.
☆ Asks whether the IDD calls could be made.
☆ Asks whether Internet is available and how much it costs to use it.
☆ Asks whether there are room services for food and drink and their prices.
☆ Thanks the floor attendant for the information.

【Situation B】 At the front office, the lobby attendant receives a couple of foreign tourists.

【Situation C】 On a certain floor, the floor attendant escorts a foreign tourist into his room.

Model 2
Making up the Room 收拾房间

Task 1

Warm-up

Work in pairs. Learn the following words about hotel services. Then answer the questions below.

disturb	towel	toilet
tidy up	turn-down service	

When a room attendant is to make up the room, what should he/she say to the guest?

Task 2

Learning Points

Listen to the following *words, phrases,* and *useful expressions* and read along. Then try to memorize them.

🔊 Words and Phrases

towel	n.	毛巾
overnight	adv.	通宵
mess	n.	混乱
cozy	adj.	舒适的，温馨的
turn-down service		做晚床（整理房间备晚上使用）

🔊 Useful Expressions

1. Should I do the turn-down service for you now?
   我现在来做晚床好吗？

2. Would you tidy up the bathroom a bit?
   请把卫生间收拾一下吧。
3. Would you like me to draw the curtains for you, sir and madam?
   我把窗帘给您拉上好吗?
4. Is there anything else I can do for you?
   还有什么我需要为您服务的?
5. We try to be always at your service.
   我们将尽力为您服务。

Task 3

🔊 Dialogue II

Listen to *Dialogue II* for the first time. Then practise the dialogue by reading it aloud with your partner. Read through it at least twice, changing your role each time.

Making up the Room

【Scene】 *The Browns are sitting in the room when a room attendant knocks at the door to see whether the turn-down service is to be done.*

A: room attendant   B: Mrs. Brown   C: Mr. Brown

A: Good evening, sir and madam. **Should I do the turn-down service for you now**?

B: Oh, thank you. But we are having some friends over to have a small party here in the room. Could you come back in three hours?

A: Certainly, madam. I'll be off at seven, but I'll let the overnight staff know. They will come then.

B: That's fine. Well, our friends seem to be a little late. **Would you tidy up the bathroom a bit**?

A: No problem.

B: Besides, please bring us a bottle of just boiled water. We'd like to treat our guests with typical Chinese tea.

A: Yes, madam. I'll bring in some fresh towels together with the drinking water.

B: OK.

A: (*Having done all as request*)

It's growing dark. **Would you like me to draw the curtains for you, sir and madam**?

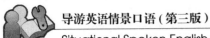

B: Why not? That would be so cozy.
A: May I turn on the lights for you?
C: Yes, please. I'd like to read short stories while waiting.
A: Yes, sir. **Is there anything else I can do for you**?
B: Nothing more. Thank you very much. You're a smart boy indeed.
A: **We try to be always at your service**. Goodbye, sir and madam, and do have a very pleasant evening.

Task 4

🔊 Listen and Answer

You will hear five questions. Listen carefully and give an appropriate answer to each of them.

(1) _____
(2) _____
(3) _____
(4) _____
(5) _____

Task 5

Role-play

Act out the following dialogues.

【Situation A】 A room attendant is to make up the room for a foreign guest. They are having a conversation in the guest's room.

Room attendant:
☆ (Knocks at the door) Asks whether it is convenient to make up the room right now.
☆ Asks what the proper time to come again is.
☆ Comes at 3:00 and asks to come in for the room service.
☆ Finishes the room service and asks whether to draw the curtains.
☆ Asks whether other services are needed.
☆ Brings some boiled water and wishes good night.

Item 3 Housekeeping Service

Guest:
☆ Tells the room attendant to come later.
☆ Tells the room attendant to come at 3:00.
☆ Gives permission.
☆ Says that they will do that by themselves.
☆ Asks for some boiled water.
☆ Expresses thanks and says goodbye.

【Situation B】 Suppose you are a room attendant, consider the following questions and imagine what you will say before, during and after the room service. Discuss with your partner, and then present it by yourself.

(1) Ask whether it is convenient for you to make up the room right now.

(2) If you get a negative answer, ask what time would be convenient for you to come back.

(3) When you finish making up the room, ask whether other services are needed.

(4) If the guests complain about the delay of the room service, try to give a satisfying explanation.

Model 3
About Room Service Order 客房用餐服务

Task 1

Warm-up

Work in pairs. If you are a room attendant, how do you introduce the items of room service to the guests? Discuss with your partner.

Task 2

Learning Points

Listen to the following *words, phrases,* and *useful expressions* and read along. Then try to memorize them.

🔊 Words and Phrases

croissant	*n.*	羊角面包
donut	*n.*	炸面圈
pot	*n.*	罐，壶
extra	*adj.*	附加的，额外的
salad	*n.*	色拉
room service		（客房）用餐服务

🔊 Useful Expressions

1. What would you like to order?
   您想点些什么？
2. Would you like a cup of coffee or a pot of coffee?
   您是要一杯咖啡还是要一壶咖啡？

3. A pot costs about 20 RMB extra.
   一壶（咖啡）要多花20元人民币。
4. Our waiter will be here in around 10 minutes.
   服务生大约10分钟后给您送去。
5. Please feel free to ask.
   请尽管讲。

Task 3

🔊 Dialogue III

Listen to *Dialogue III* for the first time. Then practise the dialogue by reading it aloud with your partner. Read through it at least twice, changing your role each time.

About Room Service Order

【Scene】*Mr. Lock in Room 1608 orders his breakfast. The staff takes his order.*

S: staff   L: Mr. Lock

S: Good morning. Room service. What can I do for you?
L: Hi, I'd like to order some food for my breakfast.
S: Yes, sir. **What would you like to order?**
L: I'd like a ham and cheese croissant, a boiled egg, and a coffee.
S: **Would you like a cup of coffee or a pot of coffee?**
L: What's the difference?
S: **A pot costs about 20 RMB extra.**
L: A pot please.
S: Anything else?
L: Do you have green salads?
S: Yes, sir. Do you want one?
L: Yes, a green salad.
S: Anything else?
L: No, that's all.
S: Could I have your name?
L: Mr. Lock of Room 1608.
S: So, Mr. Lock, we'll send to Room 1608 one ham and cheese croissant, a boiled egg, a pot of coffee, and a green salad. **Our waiter will be here in around 10 minutes.** If there is anything more you may need, **please feel**

free to ask.

L: OK.

S: Thank you. I hope you'll have a good day.

Task 4

🔊 Listen and Answer

You will hear five questions. Listen carefully and give an appropriate answer to each of them.

(1) _____

(2) _____

(3) _____

(4) _____

(5) _____

Task 5

Role-play

Act out the following dialogues.

【Situation A】 A guest (Mr. Jerry) of room 2135 orders some fruit through room service. The staff of room service answers the phone call.

The staff:

☆ Answers the phone and offers help.

☆ Says that fruit orders can be made and asks what to order.

☆ Confirms the kinds and amounts of the fruit and asks if there is anything more.

☆ Asks the brand of the beer.

☆ Asks the room and name of the guest.

☆ Tells the guest to wait for about half an hour.

Mr. Jerry:

☆ Asks whether fruit can be ordered.

☆ Orders some fruit for a small party.

☆ Orders 3 kilos of bananas, 3 kilos of apples, 2 kilos of grapes, and one kilo of strawberries.

☆ Tells the staff to buy a box of the most popular local beer.

☆ Tells the name and room.

☆ Expresses thanks.

【Situation B】 A guest orders supper for his wife and himself, the staff of the room service answers the phone.

Model 4
Hotels Today 今日酒店

Task 1

Learning Points

Listen to the following *words, phrases,* and *useful expressions* and read along. Then try to memorize them.

🔊 **Words and Phrases**

generally	adv.	一般，通常
vacation	n.	假期，度假
commercial	adj.	商业的
resort	n.	胜地
seashore	n.	海岸，海滨
residential	adj.	住宅的，与居住有关的
luxurious	adj.	奢侈的，豪华的
inexpensive	adj.	便宜的，不贵的
range	n.	范围，行列
moderate	adj.	中等的，适度的

🔊 **Useful Expressions**

1. Hotels designed for business people are known as commercial hotels.
   为出差人士设计的酒店被称为商务酒店。
2. Commercial hotels are usually located in the business section of town.
   商务酒店常建在城市的商业区。
3. This (residential) is designed to meet the needs of people who want to live in a hotel for a long time.
   这种（居家）酒店是为了满足那些想在酒店长住的人们的需要。
4. Some hotels have as few as ten rooms, while others have several hundred.

一些酒店只有十来间房，一些酒店有数百间房。

5. Hotels range from the very luxurious, which charge high rates, to the small and inexpensive that fall within the price range of a large number of travelers.

   酒店的档次不同，豪华型的酒店收费很高，小的酒店和便宜的酒店能把价格定得使大部分的旅客能够接受。

Task 2

🔊 Passage Reading

Listen to the short passage for the first time. Then practise it by reading them aloud by yourself.

Hotels Today

Hotels today are quite different from those of the past. People who stay in them are generally traveling for business, or they are touring or on vacation. Therefore, hotels are designed mainly to meet the needs of one of those two groups of people. **Hotels designed for business people are known as commercial hotels**. Hotels for people on vacation are called vacation or resort hotels.

Commercial hotels are usually located in the business section of town, while resort hotels may be at the seashore, on a mountain lake, or in the desert.

In addition to these two main types, there is a third type of hotel, called a residential hotel. **This is designed to meet the needs of people who want to live in a hotel for a long time**. Inns and hotels are located in nearly every population center in the world. In the United States alone there are about thirty thousand. **Some hotels have as few as ten rooms, and others have several hundred**. Among the largest hotels in the world today are the Conrad Hilton in Chicago, Illinois, and the Russia in Moscow, each with about three thousand rooms. In every hotel, travelers find small single rooms for the use of one person; larger double rooms for the use of two people and an arrangement of two or more rooms, called suites, which can be used by a group of persons traveling together.

Hotels range from the very luxurious, which charge high rates, to the small and inexpensive that fall within the price range of a large number of travelers. The price for a suite of rooms in a luxury hotel may be $50 a day and up, while a double room in a moderate-price hotel may cost $8 or $10 a day and up.

Task 3

🔊 Listen and Answer

You will hear five questions. Listen carefully and give an appropriate answer to each of them.

(1) _____

(2) _____

(3) _____

(4) _____

(5) _____

Task 4

Oral Practice

Retell the text in your own words.

Task 5

More Oral and Listening Practice:

【Listening】Listen to the dialogues and fill in the blanks.

🔊 Listening I

A Morning Call

A: Can I help you, sir?

B: It's _____ here. Do you have _____ service?

A: Yes, would you like to have it?

B: Yes, I want to _____ tomorrow morning.

A: _____ do you want to have it?

B: At _____ tomorrow morning. I want to get up early so that I can _____.

A: Oh, I see. What kind of call would you like, _____

	or _____?
B:	By phone, I don't like to _____.
A:	Your room number, please.
B:	_____.
A:	OK, sir. Our _____ will do that for you.

🔊 Listening II

Cleaning the Room

A:	Housekeeping. May I _____?
B:	Yes, please.
A:	Good morning, sir. May I _____?
B:	No, _____. Thanks. I'm not feeling very well now. I've _____.
A:	Oh, I'm sorry _____. Shall I _____?
B:	Not necessary. I've got some medicine.
A:	Would _____?
B:	Yes, please switch on the mini jar to make me some boiled water.
A:	Yes, sir. May I replace the _____?
B:	That's very kind of you.
A:	Should I turn on the _____ light?
B:	Yes, please. I _____.

【Topics】Divide the class into groups. Choose one of the following topics to discuss in each group. Give a short report about the group's opinion after that.

1. Do you agree with the saying "A hotel is a highly organized commercial unit." ? Why or why not?

2. In the past twenty years or so, a large number of five-star hotels have been built in China. Comment on this phenomenon.

3. When you go traveling, what kind of hotel would you prefer? Why?

Item 4

Food & Beverage Service
餐饮服务

- **Model 1**
  Reserving a Table   预订餐桌

- **Model 2**
  Food & Beverage Service   餐饮服务

- **Model 3**
  The Payment   付款

- **Model 4**
  The Chinese Food   中国饮食

Model 1
Reserving a Table 预订餐桌

Task 1

Warm-up

Work in pairs. Learn the following words of the sectors of food and beverage services. Then answer the questions below.

fry	simmer	bake	roast	stew	cocktail	wine
liquor	spirits	juice	oven	wok	pot	

1. What kind of food and drink do you usually have at home?
2. Say something about the way of cooking you know.
3. Do you know the different utensils or appliance used in cooking?

Task 2

Learning Points

Listen to the following *words, phrases,* and *useful expressions* and read along. Then try to memorize them.

🔊 **Words and Phrases**

waitress	n.	女服务员
era	n.	时代，年代
vacant	adj.	空的
come over		来，过来
view of the street		街景
dress code		着装标准

Item 4 Food & Beverage Service

🔊 Useful Expressions

1. I want to reserve a table in your restaurant.
   我想在你们饭店订座。
2. For lunch or for supper?
   订午餐（的座位）还是晚餐（的座位）？
3. What time would you come over?
   你们几点来？
4. How many of you would come, sir?
   先生，请问你们几个人？
5. We're looking forward to seeing you.
   我们期待您的到来。

Task 3

🔊 Dialogue I

Listen to *Dialogue I* for the first time. Then practise the dialogue by reading it aloud with your partner. Read through it at least twice, changing your role each time.

Reserving a Table

【Scene】 *A waitress in a restaurant receives a telephone call from a customer to book a table for lunch.*

W: Waitress   C: Customer

W: Good morning. New Era Restaurant. Can I help you?
C: **I want to reserve a table in your restaurant.**
W: **For lunch or for supper?**
C: For lunch.
W: **What time would you come over?**
C: We'll arrive at around 11:30.
W: **How many of you would come, sir?**
C: We are a group of 10.
W: OK. Could I have your name, please?
C: Frank Chen.
W: We have two vacant rooms now, 306 and 502. Which one do you prefer?

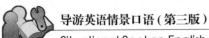

C: 502, please. We want to have a view of the street.

W: OK. Mr. Chen, you'll have a table of 10 at 502 for lunch. Do you have any dress code?

C: No. Thank you.

W: My pleasure. **We're looking forward to seeing you**.

Task 4

🔊 Listen and Answer

You will hear five questions. Listen carefully and give an appropriate answer to each of them.

(1) _____

(2) _____

(3) _____

(4) _____

(5) _____

Task 5

Role-play

Act out the following dialogues.

【Situation A】 The headwaiter of Rainbow Restaurant is receiving a telephone call from a customer to book a table. Please make a conversation with the clues offered below.

The headwaiter:

☆ Greets and tells the name of the restaurant and offers help.

☆ Asks the time the customer wants to reserve.

☆ Asks the number of the people of the reserved table.

☆ Asks the customer whether to have a smoking or a non-smoking area.

☆ Asks whether there is a dress code.

☆ Asks the name of the customer.

☆ Expresses wish to see the customer.

Item 4 Food & Beverage Service

The customer:
☆ Asks to reserve a table.
☆ Tells the headwaiter to reserve a table for supper.
☆ Says that there are seven adults.
☆ Says to prefer a non-smoking area.
☆ Tells the headwaiter there's no dress code.
☆ Tells the name.
☆ Expresses thanks.

【Situation B】 The staff of the Diamond restaurant receives a telephone call to reserve a table for 7:00. But there is no vacant table at that time. So they ask the customer whether they would reserve a table for 8:00. The customer gives a positive reply.

Model 2
Food & Beverage Service 餐饮服务

Task 1

Warm-up

Work in pairs. Learn the following words and answer the questions below.

chicken	duck	mutton	beef	seafood	fish
tomato	potato		bamboo shoots	pickles	

What kind of food do you like to have in a restaurant?

Task 2

Learning Points

Listen to the following *words, phrases,* and *useful expressions* and read along. Then try to memorize them.

🔊 Words and Phrases

vegetarian	n.	素食者
noodle	n.	面条
requirement	n.	要求
seafood	n.	海鲜
record	n.	记录
seat	n.	座位
instruction	n.	指示
beverage	n.	酒水饮料
include	v.	包括

fee	n.	费用
sofa	n.	沙发
hot dish		热菜
private room		包厢

🔊 Useful Expressions

1. Ten days ago, we reserved the meals for a tour group tomorrow.
   我们在 10 天前已预订了明天的团队餐。
2. Could you tell us the details about the reservation?
   您可以把明天用餐的具体要求说明一下吗?
3. So you should prepare vegetable dishes for them.
   请你为他们准备素菜。
4. It is located at the most flourishing place in Ningbo and is famous for seafood.
   它位于宁波商业繁华地带，是当地著名的海鲜酒楼。
5. We have arranged well for your meals in the private room named "Venice".
   我们已经做好了安排，给你们安排在"威尼斯"包间。
6. We have prepared foods for them according to your requirement.
   我们已经按照您的要求专门为他们备餐了。
7. Please take your seat in order, six persons for one table.
   请大家按次序入座，6 人一桌。
8. As beverages are not included in the fees, you should pay an extra fee for them if you need.
   酒水为自费项目，大家如有需要得另外付费。
9. All the foods have been on the table.
   菜已经全部上齐。
10. After meals, you can have a rest in the sofa of the lobby.
    用过餐后，你们可在大厅的沙发上休息一下。

Task 3

🔊 Dialogue II

Listen to *Dialogue II* for the first time. Then practise the dialogue by reading it aloud with your partner. Read through it at least twice, changing your role each time.

Food & Beverage Service

【Scene】 *The tour guide Huang Lan and the tour leader James are leading a group of foreign visitors to the reserved restaurant. The restaurant manager receives them.*

M: manager   G: guide   L: leader

(*The tour guide confirms the reservation through telephone.*)

G: Hello! Is that Shipu Hotel? I am Huang Lan, the tour guide from Ningbo Youth Travel Agency. **Ten days ago, we reserved the meals for a tour group tomorrow**. Now I want to confirm the reservation.

M: Hello, Ms. Huang. **Could you tell us the details about the reservation**? I will check it again.

G: OK. Private room on the third floor at 12:00 on September 8. Six persons in total, but including two vegetarians, **so you should prepare vegetable dishes for them**. The meals include six cold dishes, ten hot dishes, two soups, and two noodles. Please arrange it as soon as possible.

M: OK. We will make an arrangement according to your requirements.

(*The restaurant manager greets the tourist group.*)

G: Ladies and gentlemen, now we are arriving at the gate of the hotel we will have meals. The hotel is Shipu Hotel. **It is located at the most flourishing place in Ningbo and is famous for seafood**.

L: It sounds great.

G: May you have delicious food! Please follow me.

G: Hello! I am Huang Lan, the tour guide from Ningbo Youth Travel Agency. This is my tourist group.

M: Hello! I am Meng Jun, the restaurant manager of this hotel. **We have arranged well for your meals in the private room named "Venice"**.

G: By the way, we have two vegetarians. Do you have records?

M: Yes, **we have prepared foods for them according to your requirement**.

G: Good.

M: Please take the tourists to the private room.

G: Attention please. Now follow me.

(*The tour guide leads all tourists to the private room.*)

G: **Please take your seat in order, six persons for one table**. The two vegetarians sit at the special seats according to the instruction as we have prepared vegetable dishes for you. **As beverages are not included in the fees, you should pay an extra fee for them if you need**.

L: OK.

G: This is Manager Meng of this restaurant. This is our leader James.

M: Hello! I hope you will enjoy the food. If you have any question, please do not hesitate to ask me.

L: OK. Thanks for your careful arrangement.
G: **All the foods have been on the table**. Please help yourselves. **After meals, you can have a rest in the sofa of the lobby**. We will gather at the gate of the hotel at 2 o'clock.
L: OK. Thank you!
M: Enjoy your meal!

Task 4

🔊 Listen and Answer

You will hear five questions. Listen carefully and give an appropriate answer to each of them.

(1) _____
(2) _____
(3) _____
(4) _____
(5) _____

Task 5

Role-play

Act out the following dialogues.

【Situation A】 The tour guide is leading a group of foreign visitors to the reserved restaurant. The restaurant manager receives them.

The guide:
☆ Confirms the reservation through telephone.
☆ Tells the time and standard of the meal.
☆ Greets the restaurant manager and introduces the tourist group.
☆ Leads the tourists to the private room.
☆ Tells beverages are not included in the fees.
☆ Tells tourists when and where to gather after meals.

The manager:
☆ Asks the details about the reservation.

☆ Tells they will make an arrangement according to the requirements.
☆ Greets the tour guide and tells that they have arranged well for meals.
☆ Greets the tour leader.
☆ Tells tourists not to hesitate to ask her any question.
☆ Wishes tourists to have a happy eating experience.

【Situation B】 Choose one of the dishes that you are familiar with to discuss and describe how it is made. Suppose your partner is a foreign guest. Make a conversation to explain the method of making the dish.

Model 3
The Payment 付款

Task 1

Warm-up

Work in pairs. If you are the waiter to collect the bill, what questions would you usually ask?

Task 2

Learning Points

Listen to the following *words, phrases,* and *useful expressions* and read along. Then try to memorize them.

🔊 **Words and Phrases**

total	*n.*	总额
cashier	*n.*	出纳，收银员
honor	*v.*	接受（信用卡付款）
password	*n.*	密码
sign	*v.*	签名
credit card		信用卡
exchange rate		汇率
Visa	*n.*	一种信用卡，音译为"维萨"
American Express		美国运通卡

🔊 **Useful Expressions**

1. The total is 182 RMB.
   总共是 182 元人民币。

2. How much is it in dollars?
   合多少美元？
3. I'll ask the cashier.
   我问一下收银员。
4. It's 26 dollars at today's exchange rate.
   按今天的汇率是 26 美元。
5. Do you honor credit cards?
   你们是否接受信用卡付款？
6. What kind of card have you got, sir?
   先生，您用的是哪种卡？
7. Would you please come over to enter the password?
   请您过来输一下密码好吗？
8. Please sign your name here.
   请在这儿签名。

Task 3

🔊 Dialogue III

Listen to *Dialogue III* for the first time. Then practise the dialogue by reading it aloud with your partner. Read through it at least twice, changing your role each time.

The Payment

【Scene】*A foreign customer is paying at a restaurant and the waiter brings the bill.*

C: customer   W: waiter

C: Waiter, may I have the bill?
W: Yes, sir. Here it is.
C: How much is it?
W: **The total is 182 RMB.**
C: Do you accept US dollars?
W: Yes, sir.
C: **How much is it in dollars**?
W: A moment please, **I'll ask the cashier. It's 26 dollars at today's exchange rate.**
C: **Do you honor credit cards**?
W: Yes. **What kind of card have you got, sir**?

Item 4 Food & Beverage Service

C: I have Visa and American Express, which do you prefer?

W: Both are OK. It's up to you. **Would you please come over to enter the password**?

C: Oh, yes.

W: Thank you. **Please sign your name here**.

C: OK.

W: Thank you.

Task 4

🔊 Listen and Answer

You will hear five questions. Listen carefully and give an appropriate answer to each of them.

(1) _____

(2) _____

(3) _____

(4) _____

(5) _____

Task 5

Role-play

Act out the following dialogues.

【Situation A】 A customer in the restaurant wants to pay the bill. Make a conversation with the clues below:

The customer:

☆ Asks the waiter to come over with the bill.

☆ Asks the total of the bill.

☆ Asks whether the restaurant accepts an American Express.

☆ Asks whether the restaurant accepts a Visa Card.

☆ Asks whether the bill can be put on the hotel bill.

☆ Tells the waiter of the room number.

The waiter:

☆ Brings the bill and gives it to the customer.

☆ Confirms the total of the bill.

☆ Tells the customer the restaurant does not accept American Express.

☆ Tells the customer that a Visa Card is not accepted either.

☆ Says that the bill can be put on the hotel bill and asks the room number of the customer.

☆ Thanks the customer and wishes them a good night.

【Situation B】 A foreigner in the restaurant wants to pay the bill. He only has credit cards, traveler's checks, and foreign currency, while the restaurant only accepts RMB or credit cards issued in China. Suppose you are the waiter, what will you do?

Model 4
The Chinese Food 中国饮食

Task 1

Learning Points

Listen to the following *words, phrases,* and *useful expressions* and read along. Then try to memorize them.

🔊 **Words and Phrases**

varied	*adj.*	各种各样的
complex	*adj.*	复杂的
culinary	*adj.*	厨房的，烹调的
appreciation	*n.*	欣赏
flavor	*n.*	味道
geographical	*adj.*	地理的，地域的
hot	*adj.*	热的，辣的
salty	*adj.*	咸的
sour	*adj.*	酸的
dispute	*n.*	争议
pungent	*adj.*	刺激的，辛辣的
greasy	*adj.*	油腻的
tender	*adj.*	嫩的
average	*adj.*	普通的
composition	*n.*	构成，组成
consume	*v.*	消费，吃
accompany	*n.*	伴随
calory	*n.*	卡路里（热量单位）
grain	*n.*	谷物，粮食
according to		根据
vary from ...to...		从……到……不等，在……到……之间

be characterized by 以……为特征

🔊 Useful Expressions

1. Great attention is paid to culinary appreciation of the food because the food should be good not only in flavor and smell, but also in color and appearance.
   人们非常注重菜肴的观赏性，不仅要求它香、味俱佳，还要色泽、外观好看。
2. Chinese food varies from place to place mainly according to geographical difference.
   中国菜肴主要是因地域不同而不同。
3. The exact number of regional cuisine is still under dispute.
   地方菜系的确切数目还存在争议。
4. Huaiyang cuisine is characterized by its sweet flavor.
   淮扬菜的特点是甜。
5. For most Chinese, about 65 percent of an average meal's calories come from grain sources instead of meat or vegetable dishes.
   对大多数中国人而言，普通饭菜65%的热量是来自米面而不是肉类和蔬菜。

Task 2

🔊 Passage Reading

Listen to the short passage for the first time. Then practise it by reading it aloud by yourself.

The Chinese Food

Four words are often used to describe Chinese food. They are "colorful", "varied", "delicious", and "complex". **Great attention is paid to culinary appreciation of the food because the food should be good not only in flavor and smell, but also in color and appearance.**

Chinese food varies from place to place mainly according to geographical difference. Some dishes are hot, some are sweet, some are salty, and others are sour. **The exact number of regional cuisine is still under dispute**, but experts agree on at least four: Sichuan, Shandong, Cantonese, and Huaiyang. Out of each cuisine, there are several types. For instance, the Shandong cuisine includes Beijing food and Shandong food. Sichuan cuisine is characterized by its hot and pungent flavoring. The features of Shandong cuisine are fresh, tasty, and not greasy. Cantonese cuisine is known for its fresh, tender, and lightly seasoned flavor. **Huaiyang cuisine is characterized by its sweet flavor.**

However, an average Chinese meal at home is quite different in composition from a Chinese banquet. At an everyday home meal, an adult may consume two small bowls of steamed rice, or a large bowl of noodles, or several pieces of steamed bread, accompanied by several meat or vegetable dishes, but not the other way round. **For most Chinese, about 65 percent of an average meal's calories come from grain sources instead of meat or vegetable dishes.**

Task 3

Listen and Answer

You will hear five questions. Listen carefully and give an appropriate answer to each of them.

(1) _____

(2) _____

(3) _____

(4) _____

(5) _____

Task 4

Oral Practice

Retell the text in your own words.

Task 5

More Oral and Listening Practice:
【Listening】Listen to the dialogues and fill in the blanks.

Listening I

Breakfast

W: Waiter   M1: Mrs. Black   M2: Mr. Black

W: Good morning, sir and madam. What would you like to have?

M1: _____ for breakfast?
W: We serve _____ and _____ breakfast.
M1: What do you serve for _____ breakfast?
W: We serve rolls with _____.
M1: What about _____ breakfast?
W: Orange or _____ juice, tea or _____, toast with butter or jam, and _____ with bacon.
M1: I'll have _____ juice, _____ and two eggs. Can I have _____ instead of bacon?
W: Certainly, madam. And you, sir?
M2: I'll have _____ my wife.

🔊 Listening II

At a Chinese Restaurant

W: Waiter　　G: Guest

W: Good evening, sir. Can I help you?
G: I'd like to _____, but I _____ about Chinese food. Can you give me some suggestions?
W: Well, there are different _____.
G: Can you give me _____?
W: Four styles of food are especially known throughout China. They are Shandong, Cantonese, Sichuan, and Huaiyang.
G: What is the Cantonese food _____?
W: It is _____.
G: How about Shandong food?
W: It's _____.
G: And what about the Huaiyang food?
W: It's _____.
G: The last one, Sichuan food is?
W: Sichuan dishes are _____.
G: Oh, really? I like hot food. _____?
W: The famous Sichuan dishes are Mapo bean curd and shredded meat in chili sauce.
G: I'll _____.

Item 4 Food & Beverage Service

【Topics】Divide the class into groups. Choose one of the following topics to discuss in each group. Give a short report about the group's opinion after that.

1. Compare the main differences between Chinese food and Western food.
2. Why is Chinese food sold abroad different from the real Chinese food in China?
3. With the society developing rapidly, people's demands for hotel services are changing. If you were a hotel manager, what other services could you offer the guests?

Item 5

☐☐☐☐

City Sightseeing and Transportation
都市观光和交通

- **Model 1**
  City Tours   都市游

- **Model 2**
  Car Rental Service   租车服务

- **Model 3**
  Xikou   溪口

Model 1
City Tours 都市游

Task 1

Warm-up

Work in pairs. Answer the questions below.

1. Shanghai is one of the most famous cities in China. Have you been to Shanghai? Which attractions impress you most?
2. Can you translate the following scenic spots into Chinese?

the Bund	the Temple of Confucius	the Dianshan Lake scenic Site
the Guyi Garden	Huangpu river Cruise	the Jade Buddha Temple
the Yuyuan Garden	Pudong New District	the Oriental Pearl Tower

Task 2

Learning Points

Listen to the following *words, phrases,* and *useful expressions* and read along. Then try to memorize them.

🔊 Words and Phrases

fame	n.	名声，声誉
deserve	v.	值得
architectural	adj.	建筑的
exhibition	n.	表现，显示
gorgeous	adj.	极好的，吸引人的
harmony	n.	融洽，协调

Item 5 City Sightseeing and Transportation

consulate	*n.*	领事馆
gather	*v.*	聚集，集拢
headquarters	*n. (pl)*	（复数）总部
financial	*adj.*	金融的，财政的
institution	*n.*	机构
shabby	*adj.*	破旧的
chest-high	*adj.*	齐胸高的
explicit	*adj.*	明了的，不言而喻的
the Bund		（上海）外滩
Oriental Manhattan		东方曼哈顿
sightseeing spot		观光点
flood prevention wall		防汛墙
sightseers' wall		观光墙
go on a cruise		乘游艇游览
on board		上船

🔊 Useful Expressions

1. It looks like the fame is well-deserved.
   名不虚传。
2. They are known as the " Exhibition of World Architectures ".
   它们以"万国建筑园"而闻名。
3. The place we are standing now is the newly built flood prevention wall.
   我们现在站的地方就是新建成的防汛墙。
4. But the newly built sightseers' wall is wider than ever and one can enjoy broader view.
   但是新建的观光墙比以前更宽，视野也更好。
5. People say it's like a bright pearl on Huangpu River.
   人们说它像黄浦江上一颗璀璨的明珠。
6. You can say that again!
   你说得对极了！
7. All aboard, please!
   请大家上船！

Task 3

🔊 Dialogue I

Listen to *Dialogue I* for the first time. Then practise the dialogue by reading it aloud with your partner. Read through it at least twice, changing your role each time.

City Tours

【Scene】 *A tour group from USA is visiting the Bund of Shanghai. The guide is talking about the Bund with the tourists.*

G: guide   T: tourist

T: This is my first trip to Shanghai, but I heard a long time ago that Shanghai is "Oriental Manhattan", and **it looks like the fame is well-deserved**. Mingbuxuchuan.

G: Wow, your Chinese is so good!

T: You're too kind. Hey, these houses are really pretty! They don't look like Chinese buildings.

G: Many people say so. These buildings have different European architectural styles. **They are known as the "Exhibition of World Architectures".**

T: They're gorgeous and in harmony with each other. Who built these buildings?

G: In the past, many foreign countries set up their consulates in this area. And the Bund also gathered the headquarters of international financial institutions in China.

T: What's that? Is it the famous Bund?

G: Yes, you're quite right. Here we are at the Bund, the most famous sightseeing spot in Shanghai. **The place we are standing now is the newly built flood prevention wall.** Do you know what it used to be?

T: We have no idea.

G: Here used to be a shabby chest-high brick wall called the "Lovers' Wall" along Huangpu River. The meaning is quite explicit, I think.

T: What a romantic place it was!

G: **But the newly built sightseers' wall is wider than ever and one can enjoy broader view.** Please turn your eyes across the river. Can you see the tower with bright "pearls"?

T: Yes, is that the TV tower? What's the name of it?

G: The Oriental Pearl TV Tower. **People say it's like a bright pearl on Huangpu River.** It is 450 meters high and is a new attraction in Shanghai.

T: What a sight the Bund is!

G: **You can say that again**! Now, ladies and gentlemen, time for us to go on a cruise on Huangpu River. **All aboard, please.**

Item 5 City Sightseeing and Transportation

Task 4

🔊 Listen and Answer

You will hear five questions. Listen carefully and give an appropriate answer to each of them.

(1) _____

(2) _____

(3) _____

(4) _____

(5) _____

Task 5

Role-play

Act out the following dialogues.

【Situation A】 John is enjoying the beautiful scenes around the Bund. The guide makes explanations.

The guide:
☆ Greets the tourists.
☆ Introduces the buildings of European architectural styles.
☆ Explains the builder.
☆ Introduces the history of the Bund.
☆ Explains the Oriental Pearl TV Tower to tourists.
☆ Tells tourists to go on a cruise on Huangpu River.

John:
☆ Says that it's the first time visiting Shanghai and knows its fame as Oriental Manhattan.
☆ Wants to know who built these buildings.
☆ Wants to know the history of the Bund.
☆ Appreciates the fascinating scenes.
☆ Wants to know the name of the TV tower.
☆ Appreciates the Bund.

【Situation B】 Suppose you are now showing your foreign tourists around your hometown and you are telling them something about the famous scenic spots and the traditional Chinese culture in your hometown.

Model 2
Car Rental Service 租车服务

Task 1

Warm-up

Work in pairs. Match the best meaning given below with the expressions that follow and talk about the advantages of the following modes of transport.

| taxi | limousine | shuttle bus | train |
| flight | metro | light rail | maglev train |

1. A plane is making a particular journey.
2. An above-ground train system.
3. A train that floats about 10mm above the guide way on a magnetic field. It is pulled by the guide way itself by changing magnetic fields.
4. A bus service that goes regularly between two places.
5. A number of connected carriages pulled by an engine along a railway line.
6. A big expensive comfortable car.
7. A car and driver that you pay to take you somewhere.
8. A railway system that runs under the ground below a city.

Task 2

Learning Points

Listen to the following *words, phrases,* and *useful expressions* and read along. Then try to memorize them.

🔊 **Words and Phrases**

rent   *v.*   出租，租用

Item 5 City Sightseeing and Transportation

activity	n.	活动
rental	n.	租赁
available	adj.	可用的，有效的
chain	n.	连锁
procedure	n.	手续
license	n.	执照
validity	n.	有效性，正确性
passport	n.	护照
visa	n.	签证
guarantor	n.	担保人
stable	adj.	稳定的
career	n.	职业
relative	n.	亲戚
Santana	n.	桑塔纳（汽车）
Passat	n.	帕萨特（汽车）
Buick	n.	别克（汽车）
Honda	n.	本田（汽车）
Toyota	n.	丰田（汽车）
BMW	n.	宝马（汽车）
Lincoln	n.	林肯（汽车）
Rolls Royce	n.	劳斯莱斯（汽车）
deposit	n.	存款，定金
charge for		索价（要价）
depend on		依赖，依靠，取决于

🔊 Useful Expressions

1. Car rental service is available in large cities like Beijing and Shanghai nowadays.
   现在像北京和上海这样的大城市里都有租车服务。
2. You have to have an international driving license.
   你得要持有国际驾照。
3. They would check the validity of your passport and visa.
   他们要核实你护照和签证的有效期。
4. Last but not least…
   最后，也是很要紧的是……
5. How much do they usually charge for a day?
   每天的收费是多少？
6. What types of cars do they provide?
   他们都有些什么车？

7. Shall I pay some deposit for the car?
   租车是不是要付定金？

Task 3

🔊 **Dialogue II**

Listen to *Dialogue II* for the first time. Then practise the dialogue by reading it aloud with your partner. Read through it at least twice, changing your role each time.

Car Rental Service

【Scene】 *A tourist wants to rent a car for his daily activities. The guide is telling him how to use the car rental service in the city.*

G: guide   T: tourist

G: Good morning, sir. May I help you?
T: I'll have a lot of business to do while I'm here. So, do you think it possible for me to rent a car for myself?
G: Yes. **Car rental service is available in large cities like Beijing and Shanghai nowadays.**
T: Really? Where and how is the service offered?
G: Well, I know some car rental companies in the city, most of which are chains.
T: That's fine. What would be the procedure?
G: Well, first of all, **you have to have an international driving license**.
T: Luckily, I've got one with me.
G: Fine. Second, **they would check the validity of your passport and visa**.
T: My visa is valid until 2033.
G: OK. **Last but not least**, a local guarantor is required, who must have a stable career and income.
T: That might be a problem. I have neither friends nor relatives here. I wonder if you…
G: Aha, you want me to be your guarantor? OK, that shouldn't be a problem.
T: Thank you very much! And **how much do they usually charge for a day**?
G: Something between 200 to 400 yuan RMB, depending on the type of car you rent.
T: **What types of cars do they provide?**

G:	Quite a lot. The Japanese Toyota, Honda, the German BMW, the American Lincoln and Ford, the British Rolls Royce, and so on.
T:	That's very kind of you. By the way, **shall I pay some deposit for the car**?
G:	Sure. About $ 1000.

Task 4

🔊 Listen and Answer

You will hear five questions. Listen carefully and give an appropriate answer to each of them.

(1) _____

(2) _____

(3) _____

(4) _____

(5) _____

Task 5

Role-play

Act out the following dialogues.

【Situation A】 You are a guide and your tourist wants to rent a car to travel by herself. Make a short dialogue with your partner on the topic of "Car Rental Service".

The guide:

☆ Greets the tourist and asks what kind of service she needs.

☆ Tells the procedure of renting a car: driving experience and available international driving license, validity of passport and visa and a local guarantor.

☆ Tells the charge of cars rental.

☆ Tells all the types of cars provided in the car rental company.

☆ Tells how much deposit should be paid.

The tourist:

☆ Tells the reason for renting a car.

☆ Asks the charge of cars rental.

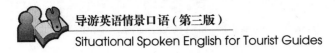
Situational Spoken English for Tourist Guides

☆ Asks the types of cars provided.
☆ Asks whether some deposit for the car should be paid.

【Situation B】 Now you are at Hangzhou and want to visit the scenic spots by bike. So you have to hire a bike.

Item 5 City Sightseeing and Transportation

Model 3
Xikou 溪口

Task 1

Learning Points

Listen to the following *words, phrases,* and *useful expressions* and read along. Then try to memorize them.

🔊 **Words and Phrases**

population	*n.*	人口
administrative	*adj.*	行政的，管理的
residence	*n.*	住处，住宅
construction	*n.*	建设，建造
consist	*v.*	组成
wing	*n.*	翅膀，翼
corridor	*n.*	走廊
traditional	*adj.*	传统的
aristocratic	*adj.*	贵族的，贵族气派的
decoration	*n.*	装饰，装饰品
application	*n.*	应用
temperament	*n.*	气质，性质，性情
Chiang Kai-shek		蒋介石
human culture		人文景观
natural scene		自然景观
lower street		下街
Shan Stream		剡溪
Bijia Hill		笔架山

🔊 Useful Expressions

1. Its human culture and natural scenery are famous both at home and abroad.
   景区内的人文景观、自然景观名扬海内外。
2. It is located at the lower street of Wuling Road in Xikou.
   它位于溪口武岭路下街。
3. In front of the house is Shan Stream which is flowing all year round.
   房前是终年潺潺不断的剡溪。
4. Its construction pattern consists of one front central room and one rear central room, two wings and four corridors. The rooms and corridors are connected with each other. It is a traditional residence of an aristocratic family.
   它的建筑格局为前后堂、两厢四廊，楼轩相接，廊庑回环，属传统的世家府第住宅。

Task 2

🔊 Passage Reading

Listen to the short passage for the first time. Then practise it by reading it aloud by yourself.

Xikou

Xikou, in Fenghua of Ningbo, is the place where Maitreya Buddha practiced his Buddhist rites, which is also the hometown of Mr. Chiang Kai-shek. Now it has become a five-star national-grade scenic spot. **Its human culture and natural scenery are famous both at home and abroad**. There are a lot of famous scenic spots, such as Fenghao House (the Former Residence of Chiang Kai-shek), Wenchang Pavilion (the Former Residence of Song Meiling), Yutai Salt Shop (the birth place of Chiang Kai-shek), the Former Residence of Jiang Jingguo, Xuedou Temple, Qianzhangyan Waterfall, Miaogao Terrace, Sanyin Pond, and so on.

Fenghao House is Chiang's former residence, also one of the key scenic spots in the state-level Xikou scenic site. **It is located at the lower street of Wuling Road in Xikou**. It faces south and looks over the street. It is named "Fenghao" and its other name is "Suju". **In front of the house is Shan Stream which is flowing all year round**. The house is also quite opposite the famous Bijia Hill. The house covers an area of 4800 square meters including a floor space of 1850 square meters. There are 49 big and small

Item 5 City Sightseeing and Transportation

rooms in it. **Its construction pattern consists of one front central room and one rear central room, two wings and four corridors. The rooms and corridors are connected with each other. It is a traditional residence of an aristocratic family.** From the history, structure, decoration, and application of Fenghao House, you can find out a lot of aspects of Chiang's world and the temperament of their life. It would be a great pleasure for a variety of visitors to see Chiang's former residence with their own eyes.

Task 3

🔊 Listen and Answer

You will hear five questions. Listen carefully and give an appropriate answer to each of them.

(1) _____
(2) _____
(3) _____
(4) _____
(5) _____

Task 4

Oral Practice

Retell the text in your own words.

Task 5

More Oral and Listening Practice:
【Listening】 Listen to the dialogue and passage and fill in the blanks.

🔊 Listening I

On the Plane

A: Ladies and gentlemen, now we're on the plane to New York. First you should find your seats and place your luggage in order. If you have any questions, you can ask me.

B: Hello, _____?

A: Of course. 20A. _____. It's a window seat.

B: Thank you. By the way, where can I put my bag?

A: _____.

B: Like this?

A: Yes, that's fine.

B: What are all these buttons and plugs in the arm rest?

A: Well, this one is the seat-recliner button. If you push the button, _____.

But for take-off and landing, the seat must be in an upright position.

B: And this one?

A: Wait. Don't push that. That's call button. If you need the stewardess for anything, _____ and she'll come to see what you need.

B: Oh, I see.

A: Sir, please don't smoke until we are airborne and the "No Smoking" sign is turned off.

B: Oh, sorry.

A: _____ and your seat is in the upright position.

B: OK. Thank you.

Listening II

Ningbo

As an old cultural city with a clear _____ of four seasons and _____ climate, Ningbo has nurtured many talented people. There are 225 _____ relics in Ningbo, among which the Hemudu Cultural Relics have a history of 7000 years. The Tianyi Building is the oldest _____ building in China. The Baoguo temple is the oldest _____ one on the upper reaches of the Yangtze River. The Yue Kiln in Shanglin is one of the origins of Chinese _____. The ancient irrigation works in Tashanyan together with the former residence of Chiang Kaishek are both important cultural relics under national _____. Besides, the Tiantong temple is the second temple to advocate Zen Sect. The Ayuwang Temple has in it the mummy of Sakyamuni. The Xuedou Temple is a _____ rite of Maitreya and a resort where people

Item 5 City Sightseeing and Transportation

pay respect to Buddhism. The Dongqian Lake is the biggest _____ lake in Zhejiang Province. These _____, together with Putuo Mountains on its east, Yandang Mountains on its south, West Lake on its west and Shanghai on its north, will definitely make Ningbo a nice place for _____ from all over the world.

【Topics】Divide the class into groups. Choose one of the following topics to discuss in each group. Give a short report about the group's opinion after that.

　　1. Most airlines now sell electronic tickets. What are their advantages and disadvantages?
　　2. What kind of life do you prefer, a busy life in big cities or a leisure and simple life in the country? Why?
　　3. Comment on the statement "Eating is the utmost important part of life" by Confucius.

Item 6

The Service of Travel Destinations
旅游目的地服务

- **Model 1**
  Narrations on Tour　沿途讲解

- **Model 2**
  At the Ticket Box　在售票处

- **Model 3**
  Asking the Way　问路

- **Model 4**
  The Role of a Tour Guide　导游的职责

Model 1
Narrations on Tour 沿途讲解

Task 1

Warm-up

Work in pairs. Try to talk about the question with your partner: "On the way to the scenic spots, as a guide, what should you tell your tourists before arriving?"

Task 2

Learning Points

Listen to the following *words, phrases,* and *useful expressions* and read along. Then try to memorize them.

🔊 **Words and Phrases**

dedicate	v.	献出
schedule	n.	时间表，一览表，计划
enlist	v.	参与，支持
UNESCO	n.	联合国教育科学文化组织
resemble	v.	相似，类似，像
serrate	adj.	锯齿状的
zigzag	v.	使成锯齿形，蜿蜒
undulate	adj.	波动的，起伏的
visible	adj.	可见的，看得见的
fortification	n.	防御工事，尤指堡垒、要塞城墙等
defense	n.	防卫，防卫物
invasion	n.	侵入，入侵
dynasty	n.	朝代，王朝

Item 6 The Service of Travel Destinations

miracle	*n.*	奇迹
belong	*v.*	属于
fit as a fiddle		精神良好，状态良好
head for		取向于
Peking Opera		京剧
The World Cultural Heritage		世界文化遗产

🔊 **Useful Expressions**

1. Can all of you hear me?
   大家都能听到我说的话吗？
2. Now we're heading for it.
   我们现在就到那儿去。
3. The tour will start at 8 o'clock and will last four hours.
   这次旅游将在 8 点开始，并持续 4 个小时。
4. And then in the evening we'll have a chance to enjoy tea at the Laoshe Teahouse and a Peking Opera is also in our schedule.
   然后在晚上，我们将有机会在老舍茶馆品茶并且欣赏京剧。
5. The Great Wall was enlisted in the World Cultural Heritage by UNESCO in 1987.
   1987 年，长城被联合国教科文组织列为世界文化遗产。
6. Before you go, please take care of your personal belongings.
   在你们出发之前，请保管好你们的私人物品。

Task 3

🔊 **Dialogue I**

Listen to *Dialogue I* for the first time. Then practise the dialogue by reading it aloud with your partner. Read through it at least twice, changing your role each time.

Narrations on Tour

G: guide   T: tourist(s)

G: Good morning, everyone! **Can all of you hear me**?
T: Yes, very clearly.
G: How are you doing today?
T: We are fit as a fiddle! Thank you!

G: So are you ready for touring?

T: Yes, of course.

G: Let's get to business. First of all, let me tell you the itinerary today. We'll start today's trip with a visit to the Great Wall. **Now we're heading for it.**

T: How long will the bus trip take to get there?

G: About half an hour. **The tour will start at 8 o'clock and will last four hours.** Then we'll have a lunch nearby. This afternoon is dedicated to the Beijing Hutong. **And then in the evening we'll have a chance to enjoy tea at the Laoshe Teahouse and a Peking Opera is also in our schedule.** I hope all of you have a wonderful trip today. Now I'd like to tell you about the Great Wall. **The Great Wall was enlisted in the World Cultural Heritage by UNESCO in 1987.** It resembles a huge, serrated wall zigzagging its way to the east and west along the undulating mountains. It is said to be visible from the moon. Sections of earlier fortifications were connected to form a united defense system against invasions from the north throughout centuries.

T: When did it take on its present form?

G: During the Ming Dynasty from 1368 to 1644.

T: It must be a great miracle!

G: Absolutely!

(Half an hour later.)

G: OK, here we are. It's time to get off the bus. **Before you go, please take care of your personal belongings.**

(They arrive at the entrance to the Great Wall.)

G: Attention, please! Now, we're going to visit the Great Wall, please do remember that we will assemble right at the main gate at 12:30. Thank you.

T: What's the number of the bus?

G: It's 288120. Have a nice trip!

Task 4

🔊 Listen and Answer

You will hear five questions. Listen carefully and give an appropriate answer to each of them.

(1) _____

(2) _____

(3) _____

(4) _____

(5) _____

Task 5

Role-play

Act out the following dialogues.

【Situation A】 The local guide is taking a group of tourists to visit the Great Wall, now they are heading for it.

Local guide:

☆ Greets everyone.

☆ Asks whether they are ready for touring.

☆ Introduces the itinerary.

☆ Tells that the bus trip will take half one hour.

☆ Gives a brief introduction of the Great Wall.

☆ Answers the tourists' questions.

☆ (When they arrive at the gate of the Great Wall), tells the tourists to take care of personal belongings and when, where they will assemble, and the number of the bus.

☆ Wishes them a nice trip.

Tourists:

☆ Greet the local guide.

☆ Express the excitement of touring.

☆ Ask how long the bus trip takes to get to the Great Wall.

☆ Ask some questions about the Great Wall, such as: its building time, its stories, and so on.

☆ Express thanks.

【Situation B】 Xiao Lu, a tour guide, is taking a group of tourists to visit Mogao Grottos, on the way to it, tourists ask some questions about the Mogao Grottos and Xiao Lu answers these questions.

Model 2
At the Ticket Box 在售票处

Task 1

Warm-up

Work in pairs. Try to translate the following words into Chinese and answer the question below.

> cultural tourism   religious tourism   historical tourism   leisure travel
> urban tourism   eco-tourism   business tourism

Which type of travel activities do you like best? Why?

Task 2

Learning Points

Listen to the following *words, phrases,* and *useful expressions* and read along. Then try to memorize them.

🔊 **Words and Phrases**

admission	n.	许可，承认
schedule	n.	行程表
memorial	adj.	记忆的
the all-in-one package		套价
Shen's Garden		沈园
Orchid Pavilion		兰亭
Temple and Tomb of Yu The Great		大禹陵
East Lake		东湖

Item 6 The Service of Travel Destinations

Sanwei Study 三味书屋

🔊 **Useful Expressions**

1. We offer the all-in-one package.
   我们提供套票。
2. What can I expect to see at these places?
   在这些地方我能看到什么？
3. They are free.
   它们是免费的。
4. RMB 20 yuan for each.
   每张票售价 20 元人民币。
5. Here are the tickets.
   给您票。

Task 3

🔊 **Dialogue II**

Listen to *Dialogue II* for the first time. Then practise the dialogue by reading it aloud with your partner. Read through it at least twice, changing your role each time.

At the Ticket Box

【Scene】 At the ticket box, the ticket clerk is answering the enquiries of a tourist.

S: staff   T: tourist

S: Welcome to the hometown of Lu Xun, Shaoxing.
T: I'd like two tickets, please.
S: OK. **We offer the all-in-one package**.
T: What does the package include?
S: You pay once for all the four scenic spots and services.
T: **What can I expect to see at these places**?
S: You may visit the Lu Xun Memorial Hall, Lu Xun Former Residence, Sanwei Study, and Hundred-Plant Garden.
T: Sounds interesting. What about other sights? Do I need to pay extra for them?
S: Yes, I'm afraid so. You can also enjoy the beautiful scenes in Shen's Garden,

Orchid Pavilion, Temple and Tomb of Yu the great and East Lake.

T: I see. Can you give me a program schedule and a map?
S: Here you are. **They are free**.
T: How much is each ticket?
S: **RMB 20 yuan for each**. Did you say you need two?
T: Yes, here is the money.
S: Thank you, sir. **Here are the tickets**. Have a nice day.

Task 4

🔊 Listen and Answer

You will hear five questions. Listen carefully and give an appropriate answer to each of them.

(1) _____

(2) _____

(3) _____

(4) _____

(5) _____

Task 5

Role-play

Act out the following dialogues.

【Situation A】A couple arrive at the ticket box located at the main entrance to the Putuo Mountain.

Staff:

☆ Greets the couple.

☆ Introduces the scenic spots.

☆ Offers the price of each ticket.

☆ Recommends restaurants.

☆ Shows the location of a bank nearby.

Tourist:

☆ Wishes to buy two tickets.

Item 6 The Service of Travel Destinations

☆ Asks what they can see.
☆ Wants to know the price of the ticket.
☆ Asks about where to dine.
☆ Wants to know where to draw money from their bank account.

【Situation B】 You are a guide and take a group of tourists to visit the Palace Museum. At the ticket box, you should buy tickets for them.

Model 3
Asking the Way 问路

Task 1

Warm-up

Work in pairs. You have just arrived at a city's railway station. Please tell your partner how to get to the hotel.

Subway Station		Post Office		Railway Station
		Strawberry Street		
Hotel	Garden	People's Square	Sun	Police Station
	Street	Grand Street	Street	
Bus Stop		Hospital		School

Task 2

Learning Points

Listen to the following *words*, *phrases*, and *useful expressions* and read along. Then try to memorize them.

🔊 Words and Phrases

stop	n.	车站
sign	n.	标记
opposite side		对面
subway station		地铁

peak time 高峰期

🔊 **Useful Expressions**

1. Could you please tell me how to go to Baoguo Temple?
   你可以告诉我保国寺怎么去吗？
2. Where is the bus station for bus No.10?
   10路公共汽车的车站在什么地方？
3. Just on the opposite side of the street.
   就在街对面。
4. Keep going straight along the road until you see the big blue subway sign.
   沿着这条街直走下去，直到你看到那个大的蓝色地铁标志。

Task 3

🔊 **Dialogue III**

Listen to the *dialogue III* for the first time. Then practise the dialogue by reading it aloud with your partner. Read through it at least twice, changing your role each time.

Asking the Way

T: *tourist*　　P: *passerby*

T: Excuse me, **could you please tell me how to go to Baoguo Temple**?
P: Sure. It's not very far from here. You can take bus No. 10 and get off at the second stop, it's two stops away.
T: I see. **Where is the bus station for bus No.10**?
P: **Just on the opposite side of the street**. Do you see where there are a lot of people waiting? There it is.
T: But it is 5 o'clock in the afternoon, there may be no bus.
P: Yes, you're right. So you can take the subway.
T: By the way, where's the subway station?
P: The subway station is a little further. Cross the street, turn around, and take the first turning on the right. **Keep going straight along the road until you see the big blue subway sign**. There it is.
T: How long does it take to get there?
P: Oh, you can walk from here within 20 minutes.

T: That' fine. Then I would rather take the subway at such a peak time. Thank you so much.

P: You're welcome.

Task 4

🔊 **Listen and Answer**

You will hear five questions. Listen carefully and give an appropriate answer to each of them.

(1) _____

(2) _____

(3) _____

(4) _____

(5) _____

Task 5

Role-play

Act out the following dialogues.

【Situation A】 Work in a group of two or three, use the following map as a guide, and make up conversations asking the way and giving directions.

Renming University of China	Zhongguancun Street	Beijing Modern Plaza
Third Ring North Road		To Airport
Beijing Friendship Hotel Beijing Institute of Technology Minzu University of China	Zhongguancun South Street	Shuang'an Department Store Capital Gym Beijing Zoo To Tian'anmen

Model 4
The Role of a Tour Guide 导游的职责

Task 1

Learning Points

Listen to the following *words, phrases,* and *useful expressions* and read along. Then try to memorize them.

🔊 Words and Phrases

ensure	*v.*	确保，保证
maximum	*adj.*	最多的，最大极限
satisfaction	*n.*	满意
particular	*adj.*	独特的，特别的，挑剔的
supervise	*v.*	监督，管理，指导
complaint	*n.*	抱怨
coordinate	*v.*	协调，整合
co-operation	*n.*	合作，协作
supplement	*n.*	补充
accurate	*adj.*	准确的，精确的

🔊 Useful Expressions

1. The tour guide should do everything possible to ensure that tour members obtain the maximum enjoyment and satisfaction from the tour.
   导游应该竭尽所能确保每一位游客在旅行中获得最大程度的享受和满足。

2. The tour guide should pay particular attention to the health and safety of the tour members.
   导游应该尤为关注游客的健康和安全。

3. Do everything possible to become knowledgeable about the cities and sites included in the itinerary of each trip he/she leads.
   导游应该竭尽所能对每一次行程所涉及的城市和景点有足够的了解。

Task 2

🔊 **Learning Points**

Listen to the short passage for the first time. Then practise it by reading it aloud by yourself.

The Role of a Tour Guide

(1) **The tour guide should do everything possible to ensure that tour members obtain the maximum enjoyment and satisfaction from the tour.**

(2) **The tour guide should pay particular attention to the health and safety of the tour members.**

(3) The tour guide should supervise the transporting of the tour members' luggage.

(4) Assist the tour members in their dealings with airlines, hotels, and other principals. For example, if a tour member's luggage is lost or damaged, help the tour member file a complaint with the airline or the department connected.

(5) Coordinate all arrangements in co-operation with the hotels and local tour guide(s). If a tour member needs a single room on his/her own, the tour guide should check the hotel first and pay a single supplement on the spot.

(6) **Do everything possible to become knowledgeable about the cities and sites included in the itinerary of each trip he/she leads.**

(7) File complete and accurate trip reports.

Task 3

🔊 **Listen and Answer**

You will hear five questions. Listen carefully and give an appropriate answer to each of them.

(1) _____

(2) _____

(3) _____

(4) _____

(5) _____

Task 4

Oral Practice

Retell the text in your own words.

Task 5

More Oral and Listening Practice:
【Listening】 Listen to the dialogue and passage and fill in the blanks.

🔊 Listening I

How to get to People's Square?

T: tourist   S: staff

T: Excuse me, _____?
S: By subway or by bus?
T: _____?
S: At this time of day, _____.
     It takes about 10 to 20 minutes. Would you like directions?
T: That would be most helpful. Thanks.
S: Sure, my pleasure. _____,
     right on the corner of Huaihai Road. You will see the signs with a red "H".
     Take _____ the
     People's Square Station.
T: _____. Thank you.
S: You're welcome. Hope you will enjoy your day.

🔊 Listening II

The Global Concept of Tour Guide Service

The global _____ of tour guide service _____ 7 meanings

represented by the word "SERVICE" with 7 letters.

S: It is "smile", the tour guide should _____ smiling service.

E: Excellent. Service should be _____ in an excellent way.

R: Ready. The tour guide is constantly _____ to serve tourists.

V: Viewing. Each tourist should be _____ as a _____ guest requiring his or her _____ care.

I: Inviting. Tourists will be invited to _____ after he/she leaves the city or the country.

C: Creating. The tour guide should create an amiable and _____ environment for tourists.

E: Eye. Each tour guide pays a close _____ to tourists with keen _____, anticipates their needs, and provides his or her service in time which makes tourists feel that they are _____ and constantly _____ by the tour guide.

【Topics】Divide the class into groups. Choose one of the following topics to discuss in each group. Give a short report about the group's opinion after that.

1. Why should a foreign traveler have proper reasons to apply for visa extension?

2. Can you describe your experience of showing a classmate or relative around your hometown? What problems did you come across and how did you solve them?

3. What influences have the philosophies of Confucianism, Taoism, yin and yang exerted on the development of Chinese culinary arts respectively?

Item 7

☐☐☐☐

Tour of Gardens　园林游览

- **Model 1**
  A Trip to the Yuyuan Garden　游览豫园

- **Model 2**
  Touring the Summer Palace　游览颐和园

- **Model 3**
  The Four Elements in a Traditional Garden　园林四要素

- **Model 4**
  Suzhou Gardens　苏州园林

Model 1
A Trip to the Yuyuan Garden 游览豫园

Task 1

Warm-up

Work in pairs. In this item, we are going to take trips to different gardens in China. First let's carry out a brief discussion.

1. Discuss the standards by which Chinese gardens can be classified.

> ☆ Contents of gardens
> ☆ Owners of gardens
> ☆ Geographical location of gardens

2. Can you translate the following gardens into Chinese and tell each other where they are located.

The Yuyuan Garden	The Summer Palace
The Chengde Mountain Summer Resort	The Humble Administrator's Garden
The Lingering Garden	The Garden of Perfection and Brightness
The Lion Forest Garden	The Master-of-Nets Garden
The Retreat and Reflection Garden	The Grand View Garden

3. Can you say something about the Yuyuan Garden? And what type of garden does the Yuyuan Garden belong to?

Task 2

Learning Points

Listen to the following *words, phrases,* and *useful expressions* and read along. Then try to memorize them.

🔊 Words and Phrases

backpacker	*n.*	背包客，背包徒步旅行者
arched	*adj.*	拱形的
ingenious	*adj.*	精巧的，敏捷的
architecture	*n.*	建筑
layout	*n.*	布局，设计
private	*adj.*	私人的
pavilion	*n.*	亭子
rockery	*n.*	假山，石园林
particularity	*n.*	特别之处
peculiar	*adj.*	特殊的
announcement	*n.*	宣告，通告
imperialist	*n.*	帝国主义者
uprising	*n.*	起义，暴动
patriotic	*adj.*	爱国主义的，爱国的
be characteristic of		具有……的特征
arched bridges		拱桥
twisting corridors and passages		回廊
the Hall for Summoning Spring		点春堂
the Small Sword Society		小刀会

🔊 Useful Expressions

1. Many tourists are attracted by its ingenious architecture and layout.
   许多游客被它独特的建筑风格和奇异的布局所吸引。
2. The buildings in the garden are characteristic of South China's style of the Ming and Qing dynasties.
   豫园的建筑具有明清时期江南地区园林的典型特征。
3. The rock looks somewhat different from the ordinary rocks.
   这块岩石看起来和普通石头有点不同。
4. The rock has four particularities.
   这块石头有四个特别之处。
5. It sounds instructive and patriotic.
   它听上去具有教育意义和爱国情怀。

Task 3

🔊 **Dialogue I**

Listen to *Dialogue I* for the first time. Then practise the dialogue by reading them aloud with your partner. Read through it at least twice, changing your role each time.

A Trip to the Yuyuan Garden

【Scene】 *Miss Zhang is a guide from the Youth Travel Service; Jack is a foreign tourist. Miss Zhang is showing Jack around the Yuyuan Garden. Jack has a special interest in the ancient Chinese gardens.*

A: Miss Zhang   B: Jack

A: Jack, I know you are a backpacker. You may walk around the Yuyuan Garden yourself. Why do you want me to travel with you?

B: Well, you know, I'm from Canada. I want to know more about this garden. Besides, I don't want to only take photos.

A: The Yuyuan Garden is a very famous classical garden, a private garden of peace and comfort in meaning. Though the garden is not very large, **many tourists are attracted by its ingenious architecture and layout**.

B: A private garden! Who built it?

A: Pan Yunduan, a governor of Sichuan Province in the Ming Dynasty, built it to bring happiness and pleasure to his parents in their old age.

B: When was it constructed?

A: The building of the garden began in 1559 and was completed in 1577. It has a history of more than four centuries.

B: It's very attractive.

A: Yes. There are more than thirty different fascinating scenes in it. Look, pavilions, towers, rockeries and goldfish ponds are connected by arched bridges and twisting corridors and passages. **The buildings in the garden are characteristic of South China's style of the Ming and Qing dynasties**.

B: It's very special and graceful. I'm very interested.

A: Yes, you are right. Look, here is a special rock named Yu Linglong (the Exquisite Jade Rock). It is one of the most famous scenic spots in the Yuyuan Garden.

B: **The rock looks somewhat different from the ordinary rocks.**

A: Yes. **The rock has four particularities.**

B: What are they?
A: First, the rock has many holes in it. Second, its absorptive capacity is excellent. Third, it has good quality and finally, its construction is peculiar.
B: How marvelous! I have never seen such a wonderful rock before. I'll take some pictures.
A: Jack, we're coming to the Hall for Summoning Spring, another important scene in the garden. It was once used as the headquarters of the Small Sword Society in 1853. The Small Sword Society was an uprising against the foreign imperialists in Shanghai.
B: Well, **it sounds instructive and patriotic**.

Task 4

Listen and Answer

You will hear five questions. Listen carefully and give an appropriate answer to each of them.

(1) _____
(2) _____
(3) _____
(4) _____
(5) _____

Task 5

Role-play

Act out the following dialogues.

【Situation A】 Mr. Wang is a tour guide who is showing a team of tourists from Australia around the Yuyuan Garden.

Mr. Wang:
☆ Greets the tourists.
☆ Introduces the history of the Yuyuan Garden.
☆ Explains the ingenious architecture and layout.
☆ Explains Yu Linglong to tourists.

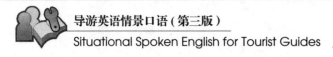

☆ Explains the Hall for Summoning Spring.

Tourists:

☆ Want to know the history of the Yuyuan Garden.

☆ Take pictures with the garden's gate as a background.

☆ Appreciate the fascinating scenes.

☆ Appreciate Yu Linglong.

☆ Give exciting remarks.

【**Situation B**】 Suppose you are a tour guide to accompany a group of tourists to visit the Chengde Mountain Summer Resort. Make up a simulated dialogue.

Model 2
Touring the Summer Palace　游览颐和园

Task 1

Warm-up

Work in pairs and answer the questions below.

1. The Summer Palace is one of the most famous gardens in China. Have you been to the Summer Palace? Which attractions impress you most?

2. Can you say the Chinese names of the following English Proper names concerning the Summer Palace? Can you introduce one or two scenic spots in English?

Anglo-French Allied forces, the Long Corridor	the Western Dike, the Kunming Lake
the Longevity Hill	the Palace of Benevolent Longevity
the Hall of Dispelling Clouds	the Tower of Buddhist Incense
the Garden of Harmonious Interest	the Suzhou Shopping Street

Task 2

Learning Points

Listen to the following *words, phrases,* and *useful expressions* and read along. Then try to memorize them.

◆ Words and Phrases

imperial	adj.	皇家的，皇帝的
bronze	n.	青铜
antler	n.	鹿角
hoof	n.	蹄子
hectare	n.	公顷
corridor	n.	走廊

extensive	adj.	广阔的，广泛的
summit	n.	顶峰，顶点
picturesque	adj.	如画的，美丽的
the Longevity Hill		万寿山
Kunming Lake		昆明湖
the Long Corridor		长廊
the Palace of Benevolent Longevity		仁寿殿
the Hall of Dispelling Clouds		排云殿

🔊 Useful Expressions

1. We will put ourselves completely in your hands.
   我们完全听从你的安排。
2. Would you please take a photo of me here?
   请在这儿给我拍张照好吗?
3. It was believed that the animal could detect the disloyal persons, preventing them from entering.
   据说这种动物能够识别不忠诚的人，不让他们入内。
4. The Summer Palace is the best-preserved and largest imperial garden in China.
   颐和园是中国保存最完整、最大的皇家园林。
5. I'm afraid one day is not enough to see all the places of interest.
   恐怕一天是看不完所有的景观的。
6. We can have an extensive view of all the fascinating places.
   所有景色一览无余。
7. What fun it is for us to row boats on the lake!
   湖上泛舟该多惬意呀!
8. After the short break, we will go to some other places worth visiting.
   短暂休息后，我们去别的值得一看的地方。

Task 3

🔊 Dialogue II

Listen to *Dialogue II* for the first time. Then practise the dialogue by reading them aloud with your partner. Read through it at least twice, changing your role each time.

Touring the Summer Palace

【Scene】 *Miss Liu, the tour guide, is leading a tour group into the Summer Palace for the visit.*

Item 7 Tour of Gardens

A: Miss Liu   B: tourists

A: Good morning, everyone. Today we are going to tour the Summer Palace, a very famous imperial garden in China.

B: All right. **We will put ourselves completely in your hands**.

A: Here we are. This is the Summer Palace.

B: Oh, the gate with one bronze lion on each side looks very magnificent. **Would you please take a photo of me here**?

A: Sure. Say "cheer"! OK. Please look at the bronze animal. This animal is peculiar because it has the head of a dragon, the antlers of a deer, the tail of a lion, and the hooves of an ox.

B: So interesting. What functions does it have?

A: **It was believed that the animal could detect the disloyal persons, preventing them from entering**.

B: What a big garden! Can you tell us some information on it, Miss Liu?

A: Of course. **The Summer Palace is the best-preserved and largest imperial garden in China**. It covers an area of 290 hectares and has many palaces, pavilions, bridges, and corridors in it.

B: Wonderful. **I'm afraid one day is not enough to see all the places of interest**. Where should we go first?

A: In the Summer Palace, there are mainly three parts: palaces for political activities, religious buildings, and the living area. First let's climb the hill. This way please.

B: We're nearly on the top of the hill. Now, **we can have an extensive view of all the fascinating places**.

A: Wow, we succeeded in coming to the summit of the Longevity Hill. Look. That is the Kunming Lake. It is picturesque. The lake is man-made and covers three-fourths of this garden.

B: What a lovely view! **What fun it is for us to row boats on the lake**! Can we take a boat ride?

A: Of course, you can. Would you like to have a rest in that pavilion?

B: That's a good idea!

A: **After the short break, we will go to some other places worth visiting**, for example, the Long Corridor, the Palace of Benevolent Longevity, the Hall of Dispelling Clouds.

B: All right, we'll follow you.

Task 4

🔊 Listen and Answer

You will hear five questions. Listen carefully and give an appropriate answer to each of them.

(1) _____

(2) _____

(3) _____

(4) _____

(5) _____

Task 5

Role-play

Act out the following dialogues.

【Situation A】 Miss Deng is a tour guide who is leading a tour group of Canadian tourists in the Summer Palace. You are asked to act out a dialogue according to the following tips.

Miss Deng:
☆ Greets the tourists.
☆ Introduces today's itinerary.
☆ Interprets the lion at the gate of the Summer Palace.
☆ Explains the peculiar bronze animal to the tourists.
☆ Interprets the Longevity Hill.
☆ Explains Kunming Lake and other scenic attractions.

Tourists:
☆ Greet the tour guide, Miss Deng.
☆ Ask to take a picture.
☆ Ask the tour guide for some basic information about the Summer Palace.
☆ Give excited remarks on the top of the Longevity Hill.
☆ Suggest rowing boats on Kunming Lake.
☆ Visit other scenic attractions.

Item 7 Tour of Gardens

【Situation B】 Suppose you are an English tour guide and will usher your American friend George to visit the Forbidden City.

Tour guide:

☆ This is the world-famous Forbidden City where emperors and their families lived.

☆ 24 emperors of the Ming and Qing Dynasties. It was first built in 1406, the Ming Dynasty.

☆ It is the largest and best-preserved palace complex in China and one of the most magnificent ancient palace complexes in the world. The entire building complex can be divided into two parts: the inner palaces and the outer palaces.

☆ They have different functions. The inner palaces were the emperors' residential area while the outer palaces were places to handle state affairs.

☆ It's called the Hall of Supreme Harmony, which is the most spectacular of all the palace buildings and also the largest hall built entirely of wood in China. It's one of the three halls of the outer palaces that are the Hall of Supreme Harmony（太和殿）, the Hall of Complete Harmony（中和殿）, and the Hall of Central Harmony（保和殿）.

☆ It was the most important place for emperors to handle all official business. Ceremonies such as grand celebration and emperor's birthday all took place here.

☆ Yes. The throne symbolized the supreme power of the feudal emperors.

George:

☆ How many emperors once lived here?

☆ Wow, 24 emperors! Though it has a history of over 500 years, it still looks elaborate and picturesque.

☆ What are the differences between them?

☆ I see. What's the grand hall?

☆ What's the use of the Hall of Supreme Harmony?

☆ Is that the emperor's throne on top of the platform?

【Situation C】 You are a guide and you are required to make up a dialogue to introduce the Long Corridor in the Summer Palace to the tourists.

Model 3
The Four Elements in a Traditional Garden
园林四要素

Task 1

Warm-up

Work in pairs. Suppose you are a guide, and you are going to introduce major elements of a classical garden and their functions to your guests, what will you say to them? Discuss with your partner.

Task 2

Learning Points

Listen to the following *words, phrases,* and *useful expressions* and read along. Then try to memorize them.

🔊 Words and Phrases

imitation	n.	仿制品
microcosm	n.	微观世界
landscape	n.	风景，景色
architecture	n.	建筑
artificial	adj.	人造的，人工的
fountain	n.	喷泉
insight	n.	洞察力，见识
lively	adj.	活泼的，生气勃勃的
symbolize	vt.	象征
longevity	n.	长寿，长命
perseverance	n.	坚持不懈

endurance	n.	忍耐力
clean-handedness	n.	清廉
lotus	n.	荷花，莲花
harmonious	adj.	和谐的
man of letters		文人，学者
outstanding feature		突出特点

🔊 Useful Expressions

1. I have got the impression that many Chinese gardens have a similar pattern.
   在我的印象中，许多中国园林的模式很相似。
2. A classical garden should include the four basic elements: mountains, waters, plants, and architecture.
   传统园林的四要素包括山石、水体、植物和建筑。
3. The rockery built of individual stones is one of the most outstanding features of the Chinese garden.
   由石头堆成的假山是中国园林最突出的特点之一。
4. Water is the central element for it provides movement, coolness and sounds within the garden.
   水是园林的关键因素，能给园林带来动感、凉爽和声音。
5. I'm beginning to get an insight into your "mountain and water culture".
   我开始了解你们的山水文化了。
6. Pine trees, for instance, symbolized longevity, perseverance, and bitter endurance.
   譬如，松树象征着长寿、坚持不懈和坚韧不拔。

Task 3

🔊 Dialogue III

Listen to *Dialogue III* for the first time. Then practise the dialogue by reading it aloud with your partner. Read through it at least twice, changing your role each time.

The Four Elements in a Traditional Garden

【Scene】*Miss Wang, a tour guide, is trying to explain the four basic elements of a classical garden to the foreign tourists.*

   A: *Miss Wang*   B: *tourists from Canada.*

B: Miss Wang, **I have got the impression that many Chinese gardens have a**

similar pattern. Why is that?

A: Well, people have been following a basic principle in building a garden, which is an imitation of nature or as many people like to call it, a "microcosm of Nature".

B: You mean the landscape?

A: Not only the landscape. **A classical garden should include the four basic elements: mountains, waters, plants, and architecture**.

B: I see. But what if there is a limitation on size for a garden?

A: Then artificial hills would be piled up instead of a natural mountain. **The rockery built of individual stones is one of the most outstanding features of the Chinese garden.**

B: What about the waters?

A: The water areas, either natural or man-made, include lakes, rivers, ponds, streams, waterfalls, and fountains. **Water is the central element for it provides movement, coolness, and sounds within the garden**. In garden designing mountains and waters usually go together.

B: Yeah, **I'm beginning to get an insight into your "mountain and water culture"**.

A: Very good. Let's go on to plants, the liveliest part of a garden.

B: That is easy to understand. They can add much natural beauty to a garden.

A: Right, but more than that. The trees and flowers were carefully chosen to show the owner's special personality and preference.

B: I have no idea about that.

A: **Pine trees, for instance, symbolized longevity, perseverance and bitter endurance**. And lotus, one of the favorite flowers of man of letters in the past, represented purity, clean-handedness.

B: Thanks, Miss Wang. What about the last element, architecture?

A: Architecture is the most human part of a garden. It appears in different styles, such as a pavilion, a temple, a corridor, a tower, a bridge, and a palace, to create the harmonious man-made beauty in a garden.

B: Thanks a lot. I have a better understanding of a Chinese garden.

Task 4

🔊 Listen and Answer

You will hear five questions. Listen carefully and give an appropriate answer to each of them.

Item 7 Tour of Gardens

(1) _____

(2) _____

(3) _____

(4) _____

(5) _____

Task 5

Role-play

Act out the following dialogues.

【Situation A】 Miss Wang, a tour guide, continues to explain the four basic elements of a classical garden to the foreign tourists.

Tourists:

☆ Ask for the trees typically chosen in a traditional Chinese garden.

☆ Ask for the flowers usually planted in a garden.

☆ Ask for the animals often raised in a traditional garden.

☆ Wonder the reasons for raising animals in a garden.

☆ Want to know how architecture can be human because Miss Wang says "Architecture is the most human part of a garden".

☆ Ask for the meaning of "frustrations".

☆ Express thanks.

Miss Wang:

☆ Introduces typical trees including pine trees, bamboos, maples, and plum trees.

☆ Introduces the usual flowers: lotus flowers, peach flowers, orchid, plum flowers, and osmanthus flowers.

☆ Answers the typical animals including deer, cranes, swans, peacocks, and goldfish.

☆ Explains the reasons with examples: male and female cranes are loyal to each other until their old age; the goldfish symbolizes property and wealth.

☆ Tells the concrete reasons: the architectural buildings can reveal the level of building techniques and kinds of materials used in different periods. And the literary decorations on the buildings such as paintings, calligraphy, couplets, poems, and furniture all expressed the owner's special experiences and frustrations.

☆ Explains that many owners were retired or dismissed officials or men of letters who had never had any chances and they were seeking quiet places to escape from the "busy world", or in modern term "go back to nature".

【**Situation B**】 You are asked to discuss and make a dialogue on the representative significance of pine trees, bamboos, and plums respectively in the Chinese traditional culture.

Item 7 Tour of Gardens

Model 4
Suzhou Gardens   苏州园林

Task 1

Learning Points

Listen to the following *words, phrases,* and *useful expressions* and read along. Then try to memorize them.

🔊 Words and Phrases

paradise	n.	天堂
wonderland	n.	仙境，奇异的地方
tranquil	adj.	宁静的，平静的
exquisite	adj.	高雅的，精巧的
in good condition		保存良好的
Venice in the East		东方威尼斯
the Humble Administrator's Garden		拙政园
the Lion Forest Garden		狮子林
the Lingering Garden		留园
the Master-of-Nets Garden		网师园
the Lotus Garden		耦园
the Pavilion of the Surging Waves		沧浪亭
the Chengde Mountain Summer Resort		承德避暑山庄
the World Heritage List		世界遗产名录
Kingdom of Rockeries		假山王国

🔊 Useful Expressions

1. Suzhou is one of the oldest cultural cities in China, a place of great beauty, and a wonderland of rivers and gardens.
   苏州是中国古老的文化名城之一，风景非常优美，河流交错，园林密布。

2. The gardens south of the Yangtze River are the best under Heaven, and among them the gardens of Suzhou are the best.

   江南园林甲天下，苏州园林甲江南。

3. Suzhou is unique in terms of the number of gardens, their tranquil environment, refined layout, and exquisite building style.

   苏州的独特之处在于园林的数量、静谧的环境、精巧的布局和高雅的建筑风格。

4. The Pavilion of the Surging Waves is known for its tranquil scenery and simple architecture.

   沧浪亭以它宁静的环境和简约的建筑风格而闻名。

5. Suzhou deserves the fame of a human paradise on earth.

   苏州不愧为人间天堂！

Task 2

🔊 Passage Reading

Listen to the short passage for the first time. Then practise it by reading it aloud by yourself.

Suzhou Gardens

Suzhou is one of the oldest cultural cities in China, a place of great beauty, and a wonderland of rivers and gardens. It has always been renowned as a "paradise on earth" and the "Venice in the East". One well-known proverb says "Paradise in heaven, Suzhou and Hangzhou on earth". Another old saying goes, **"The gardens south of the Yangtze River are the best under Heaven, and among them the gardens of Suzhou are the best."**

Suzhou is unique in terms of the number of gardens, their tranquil environment, refined layout, and exquisite building style. The masterpieces of classical gardens, still in good condition, include the Humble Administrator's Garden, the Lion Forest Garden, the Lingering Garden, the Master-of-Nets Garden, the Lotus Garden, and the Pavilion of the Surging Waves. The unique charm of these gardens led to their entry into the World Heritage List in 1997 and 2000.

The Humble Administrator's Garden is one of the four classical gardens in China, together with the Summer Palace in Beijing, the Chengde Mountain Summer Resort, and the Lingering Garden in Suzhou. It's also the largest of the four famous classical gardens in Suzhou, the other three being the Pavilion of the Surging Waves, the Lion Forest Garden, and the Lingering Garden.

Item 7 Tour of Gardens

The Pavilion of the Surging Waves is known for its tranquil scenery and simple architecture. The garden has long corridors along the banks of the ponds. The Lion Forest Garden, renowned as a "Kingdom of Rockeries", is exquisite and imaginative in its design of rockeries. Stones in the garden take on different interesting shapes of lions, lying, sitting, and standing. The Lingering Garden consists of four sections: rockeries in the west, picturesque scenery in the north, hall and pavilion structures in the east, and hills and waters at the center. A winding corridor of over 700 meters links them.

Suzhou deserves the fame of a human paradise on earth.

Task 3

Listen and Answer

You will hear five questions. Listen carefully and give an appropriate answer to each of them.

(1) _____

(2) _____

(3) _____

(4) _____

(5) _____

Task 4

Oral Practice

Retell the text in your own words.

Task 5

More Oral and Listening Practice:

【Listening】 *Listen to the dialogues and fill in the blanks.*

Listening I

Touring the Grand View Garden

A: Today we are going to visit the famous Grand View Garden. Our bus will stop at a small bridge and we'll climb the nearby tower to _____ the Grand View Garden. _____. Look at these buildings with white walls and black roofs.

B: _____!

A: Yes, it is a typical garden in the south of the Yangtze River. Now we'd like to see a screen wall.

B: _____?

A: Yes, but we have to go around the screen wall.

B: Aha, why does the screen wall stand in the way?

A: _____. And it also makes it more difficult for evil spirits to enter.

B: _____.

A: _____?

B: No. I've never been to these places in China before.

A: Now we will walk through the heavy red gate and into the courtyards with unique styles. Just ahead, there is a group of strange rocks, ponds and willows. Among them is the home of Jia Baoyu, one major character of *The Story of Stones* by Cao Xueqin.

B: _____!

Listening II

Visiting the Chengde Mountain Summer Resort

A: It is said that the Chengde Mountain Summer Resort is the largest surviving imperial garden complex in China. _____ _____. Is that true?

B: Yes, it covers an area of 5.6 million square meters which is twice the size of the Summer Palace. And the mountain resort consists of a palace area and a scenery area. _____?

A: _____ since we have visited many palaces in Beijing. The palaces here are mostly made from dark hardwood. In the scenery area, there is a big lake. Lotuses and pines grow around.

B: OK. Let's go around the scenery area first. Look, _____ _____, reminding one of the land south of the

Item 7 Tour of Gardens

Yangtze River. And the water in the lake is so clear and blue.

A: The hill over there is called the Gold Hill. _____.
Standing on the top of the hill, _____
_____. Is there a spring flowing out of the cracks in the north of the Gold Hill?

B: Yes. It is called the Warm River Spring.

A: Oh, look at the peak on the east.

B: It looks like an inverted washing club, so people call it the Club Peak（棒槌峰）. It's so unique.

A: _____. This kind of beautiful scenery is rare in the north of China. I feel as if I were in a different world.

B: _____?

A: That's a good idea.

【Topics】Divide the class into groups. Choose one of the following topics to discuss in each group. Give a short report about the group's opinion after that.

1. Give a brief oral introduction to classical gardens in China such as their types, features, locations and their representative masterpieces.

2. Discuss and make a guide commentary concerning a famous garden in China.

3. What differences do you know about the table manners in China and in the Western countries?

Item 8

☐☐☐☐

Tour of Mountains　山、水之旅

- **Model 1**
  In Huangshan　黄山之旅

- **Model 2**
  A Trip in Guilin　游览桂林

- **Model 3**
  Huangguoshu Waterfall　黄果树瀑布

- **Model 4**
  West Lake　西湖

Model 1
In Huangshan 黄山之旅

Task 1

Warm-up

Work in pairs. Discuss the following questions with your partner.

1. Have you been to Mount Huangshan? Which scenic spots impress you most deeply?
2. Could you name the three main peaks and the four wonders of Mount Huangshan in English?

Task 2

Learning Points

Listen to the following *words, phrases,* and *useful expressions* and read along. Then try to memorize them.

🔊 **Words and Phrases**

odd	*adj.*	奇怪的
grotesque	*adj.*	奇形怪状的
world-renowned	*adj.*	世界闻名的
curative	*adj.*	能治病的
marvelous	*adj.*	奇妙的，了不起的
odd pines		奇松
grotesque rocks		怪石
cloud seas		云海
hot springs		温泉
the Guest-Greeting Pine		迎客松
the See-the-Guest-off Pine		送客松
the Phoenix Pine		凤凰松

Item 8 Tour of Mountains

the Black Tiger Pine 黑虎松
the Flower of a Dreaming Pen 梦笔生花
Monkey Gazing at the sea 猴子观海
the Turtle Peak 鳌鱼峰
the Five Sacred Mountains 五岳

Useful Expressions

1. Wow, what beautiful scenery! Can we get off the coach and take some pictures?
   哇，多么美丽的风景！我们下车拍些照片吧。
2. Look ahead! Have you seen pine trees on that peak with such shapely leaves?
   朝前看！你们看见山顶那些形态优美的黄山松了吗？
3. Mount Huangshan is world-renowned for its four wonders.
   黄山因"四绝"而闻名于世。
4. The Guest-Greeting Pine always stretches out its arms to welcome guests from all over the world.
   迎客松总是伸出双臂欢迎全世界的宾客。
5. The mountain's grotesque rocks are given fancy names, such as the Flower of a Dreaming Pen, Monkey Gazing at the Sea, and the Turtle Peak.
   黄山怪石被冠以奇特的名称，如梦笔生花、猴子观海、鳌鱼峰。
6. Mount Huangshan deserves the fame for "No. 1 Mountain under Heaven"!
   黄山不愧有"天下第一山"的美称。
7. One visits no mountains after the Five Sacred Mountains. And after Mount Huangshan, one has no eye for the Five Sacred Mountains.
   五岳归来不看山，黄山归来不看岳。

Task 3

Dialogue I

Listen to *Dialogue I* for the first time. Then practise the dialogue by reading it aloud with your partner. Read through it at least twice, changing your role each time.

On Huangshan

A: Miss Qin, a local tour guide   B: tourists from the Great Britain

A: Ladies and gentlemen, attention, please. We are reaching the foot of Mount

Huangshan.

B: **Wow, what beautiful scenery! Can we get off the coach and take some pictures**?

A: Sure. Now the coach has stopped. Please get off the coach one by one. **Look ahead! Have you seen pine trees on that peak with such shapely leaves**?

B: Yes, terrific! They have odd shapes.

A: As mentioned on the bus, Mount Huangshan is called "No. 1 Mountain under Heaven". **It is world-renowned for its four wonders**.

B: Four wonders? What are they?

A: Odd pines, grotesque rocks, cloud seas, and hot springs.

B: Wonderful, odd pines are unique. Are there any famous Huangshan pines?

A: Yes. More than 1,000 pines are named with different beauty and grace. Some of the most well-known pines are: the Guest-Greeting Pine, the See-the-Guest-off Pine, the Phoenix Pine, and the Black Tiger Pine.

B: The Guest-Greeting Pine is the most famous. **It always stretches out its arms to welcome guests from all over the world**.

A: Besides odd pines, **the mountain's grotesque rocks are given fancy names, such as the Flower of a Dreaming Pen, Monkey Gazing at the Sea, and the Turtle Peak**. Don't worry. I'll show you those rocks later.

B: Well, we won't miss them. What about the clouds?

A: When on the mountain, you see clouds form at any time of the day. They float, stay, or spread. Their shapes change with each step you walk. As for hot springs, the water stands at 42 degrees centigrade all year round and is said to have curative effects for some diseases.

B: That's great. **Mount Huangshan deserves the fame for "No. 1 Mountain under Heaven"**!

A: It's true. There is a famous saying like this: **"One visits no mountains after the Five Sacred Mountains. And after Mount Huangshan, one has no eye for the Five Sacred Mountains."**

B: That sounds very marvelous and exciting.

Task 4

🔊 Listen and Answer

You will hear five questions. Listen carefully and give an appropriate answer to each of them.

(1) _____

(2) _____
(3) _____
(4) _____
(5) _____

Task 5

Role-play

Act out the following dialogues.

【Situation A】 Mr. Zhang is a tour guide who is going to show a group of tourists around Mount Emei.

Mr. Zhang:

☆ Reaches the foot of Mt. Emei and sees a big archway.

☆ Introduces the Chinese characters written on the archway: a famous mountain under Heaven（天下名山）, a Buddhist Holy Land（佛教圣地）.

☆ Takes the teleferic to the Wannian Temple.

☆ Gives a legend about the Emperor Shenzong of the Ming Dynasty, who renamed the Wannian Temple to express his gratitude to his mother.

☆ Tells that the beautiful view is called the Autumn wind over the Baishui Pool, one of the ten marvels of Mt. Emei.

Tourists:

☆ Get off the coach and take pictures.

☆ Want to know its characters.

☆ Ask for the reasons for changing the Puxian Temple to the Wannian Temple.

☆ Say it is a miracle and it is very kind of Emperor Shenzong.

☆ Appreciate the beautiful scenery: the maple leaves turn red all over the mountain and the red leaves are reflected in the pool.

【Situation B】 Suppose you are a tour guide to accompany Miss Smith to tour Mount Taishan. You are required to make up a dialogue including at least the following information.

☆ The highest summit is 1545m above the sea level.

☆ Daimiao（岱庙）, the Dai Temple, the place where the God of Mt. Taishan is worshipped.

☆ Wudafu Song Ting（五大夫松亭）, the Fifth Rank Pine Pavilion, has a touching story.

☆ The Eighteen Bends（十八盘）—— the 1,000-meter-long precipitous steps to the South Heaven.

☆ Gate.

☆ Yudi Feng（玉帝峰）, the Jade Emperor Summit, is the highest peak of Mt. Taishan.

☆ The temple of Jade Emperor（玉帝庙）.

Item 8 Tour of Mountains

Model 2
A Trip in Guilin 游览桂林

Task 1

Warm-up

Work in pairs. Discuss and answer the following questions.

1. It is said that the landscape in Guilin is one of the best in the world. What are the "Four Wonders" of Guilin's landscape? And what scenic areas are more famous in Guilin?

2. Guilin is famous for its beautiful scenery. Do you know which adjective words can often be used to describe the word "scenery"?

Task 2

Learning Points

Listen to the following *words, phrases,* and *useful expressions* and read along. Then try to memorize them.

🔊 Words and Phrases

landscape	*n.*	风景，景色；风景画
karst	*n.*	喀斯特
cobble	*n.*	鹅卵石
cormorant	*n.*	鸬鹚，水老鸦
shroud	*vt.*	笼罩，覆盖
wonderland	*n.*	仙境，奇异的地方
the Lijiang River		漓江
the Elephant-Trunk Hill		象鼻山
the Folded Brocade Hill		叠彩山
the Wave-Subduing Hill		伏波山

the Reed Flute Cave	芦笛岩
the Seven-Star Cave	七星岩
the Solitary Beauty Peak	独秀峰
the Nine-Horse Hill	九马画山

🔊 Useful Expressions

1. Guilin's landscape is second to none./ Guilin has the finest mountains and rivers under heaven.
   桂林山水甲天下。
2. Guilin's landscape is noted for its green hills, elegant rivers, strange caves, and beautiful rocks.
   桂林山水以山青、水秀、洞奇、石美而著称。
3. To be an immortal is not as good as to be an ordinary person living in Guilin.
   愿作桂林人，不愿作神仙。
4. We are eager to appreciate the unique scenery with our own eyes.
   我们急切地想饱览别具一格的美景。
5. The water of the Lijiang River is so clear and pure that you can see the cobbles on the bottom.
   漓江的水多清澈，连江底的鹅卵石都可以看得见。
6. Fantastic! I feel as if I'm in a wonderland.
   美极了！我好像置身仙境了。
7. What a beautiful sculpture of nature!
   多美的天然雕刻啊！

Task 3

🔊 Dialogue II

Listen to *Dialogue II* for the first time. Then practise the dialogue by reading it aloud with your partner. Read through it at least twice, changing your role each time.

A Trip in Guilin

A: a tour guide   B: tourists

A: Ladies and gentlemen, today we are going to tour Guilin, a world-renowned scenic city and an excellent tourist city in China.

B: Great. **Guilin's landscape is second to none.** Could you give us a brief introduction to Guilin?

A: Yeah. Because of a typical karst formation, **Guilin's landscape is noted for its green hills, elegant rivers, strange caves, and beautiful rocks.** Guilin has the finest mountains and rivers under heaven. Some people even say, **"To be an immortal is not as good as to be an ordinary person living in Guilin."**

B: Marvelous. **We are eager to appreciate the unique scenery with our own eyes.** What are the famous scenic areas in Guilin?

A: They are the Lijiang River, the Elephant-Trunk Hill, the Folded Brocade Hill, the Wave-Subduing Hill, the Reed Flute Cave, the Seven-Star Cave, and the Solitary Beauty Peak.

B: Which scenic spot should we visit first?

A: The Lijiang River, one of the most famous scenic spots in Guilin. Let's go.

B: All right.

(*The guide and the tourists are cruising on the Lijiang River to Yangshuo.*)

B: Look! **The water of the Lijiang River is so clear and pure that you can see the cobbles on the bottom.**

A: Yes. The reflection of the hills in the water looks so real and the farmlands stretch out like green carpets. They form magnificent scenery on earth.

B: **Fantastic! I feel as if I'm in a wonderland.**

A: Yes, the beautiful landscapes of Guilin have inspired painters for centuries. What's more, you'll enjoy another kind of fascinating view when you come on a rainy day. The hills are shrouded in mist. The water is clearer and the hills are greener.

B: There! The hill looks like an elephant. I remember seeing it somewhere.

A: It is the Elephant Trunk Hill. It looks like an elephant drinking water with its long trunk.

B: **What a beautiful sculpture of nature!** Look there. A fisherman is fishing on a bamboo raft and his cormorants are busy catching fish. What a fascinating scene!

A: That is a traditional way of fishing in Guilin. It is one of the things that attracts tourists to Guilin.

B: I am greatly impressed by it.

A: Pretty soon we will see another wonder along the Lijiang River, the Nine-Horse Hill.

B: Why is it called the Nine-Horse Hill? Are there nine horses on it?

A: Yes, you are right. It is named because there is a saying that if you are clever enough you can find nine horses of different shapes on the cliff.

B: I see. I'll try to be clever by finding as many horses as possible.

Task 4

🔊 Listen and Answer

You will hear five questions. Listen carefully and give an appropriate answer to each of them.

(1) _____

(2) _____

(3) _____

(4) _____

(5) _____

Task 5

Role-play

Act out the following dialogues.

【Situation A】 Miss Wang, a tour guide, answers some questions by tourists who have great interest in the Jiuzhaigou Valley.

Miss Wang:

☆ Confirms the tourist's opinion that Jiuzhaigou's waterscape is better than Guilin's.

☆ Says there are five wonders: emerald lakes, layered waterfalls, colorful forests, snow-clad peaks, and Tibetan customs.

☆ Says that the tour includes the chance to visit the Tibetan villages.

☆ Tells that water is the soul of the Jiuzhaigou Valley and it has 108 lakes, 47 springs, and 17 waterfalls.

☆ Says that all are fascinating and the Nuorilang Waterfall is a landmark.

☆ Tells that tourists can see rainbows when the sun is shining in the summer.

Tourists:

☆ Think the waterscape of Jiuzhaigou is better than that of Guilin.

☆ Ask which wonders to see in the Jiuzhaigou Valley.

☆ Tell that they have special interest in Tibetan customs.

☆ Ask which is the most typical.

☆ Ask which is the most beautiful one among plenty of waterscape.

☆ Ask whether they can see rainbows above the waterfalls.

【**Situation B**】 A tour group is touring Lake Taihu. Please have a dialogue between a tour guide and tourists according to the information given below.

A tour guide:

☆ The Tortoise Head Garden is the best place to appreciate the beauty of Lake Taihu.

☆ The place is like a tortoise sticking out its head into the lake to drink water.

☆ They mean the Tortoise Head Garden.

☆ The wind is not strong and the waves are not big. If the wind is up, huge waves will roar.

☆ The lake often offers you a picturesque scene whether you look near or far.

☆ There are three hills or islands in Lake Taihu. The one in the center is called the Drum Hill. The other two are called the East Duck and the West Duck, because they are shaped like ducks.

☆ Let's go.

Tourists:

☆ Why is it called the Tortoise Head Garden?

☆ See three big Chinese characters, what do they mean?

☆ Hear the rumbling surging waves.

☆ That should be spectacular.

☆ What a vast lake! How freely the birds fly!

☆ There are some hills in the lake.

☆ Can we go to the hills?

Model 3
Huangguoshu Waterfall 黄果树瀑布

Task 1

Warm-up

Work in pairs. Discuss and answer the following questions.

1. Have you been to Huangguoshu Waterfall before? Where is it and what's special about Huangguoshu Waterfall?

2. Could you make a comparison between Huangguoshu Waterfall and a waterfall you have ever seen?

Task 2

Learning Points

Listen to the following *words, phrases,* and *useful expressions* and read along. Then try to memorize them.

🔊 Words and Phrases

rough	*adj.*	汹涌的，吵闹的
thunderous	*adj.*	轰隆般的，打雷似的
roar	*v.*	咆哮，轰鸣
refraction	*n.*	折射
arch	*v.*	拱起，变成弓形
float	*v.*	漂浮，漂流
gallop	*v.*	飞奔
Huangguoshu Waterfall		黄果树瀑布
karst landform		喀斯特地形
the Water-Curtain Cave		水帘洞

the Milky Way	银河
the Rhinoceros Pool	犀牛潭
the Water-Viewing Pavilion	观水亭

🔊 Useful Expressions

1. Huangguoshu Waterfall is the largest waterfall in China, 78 meters high and 101 meters wide.
   黄果树瀑布高78米、宽101米，是中国最大的瀑布。
2. Huangguoshu Waterfall is listed in the national park of China.
   黄果树瀑布被列入中国国家级风景名胜区。
3. The waterfall looks just like a huge curtain hanging in front of the cave.
   洞前的瀑布犹如一幅巨大的水帘。
4. You may feel as if bunches of pearls and silver chains are falling upon you.
   你会感觉到串串水珠、银色水链飞溅在身上。
5. What a grand and attractive scene!
   多么壮观和扣人心弦的景色呀！

Task 3

🔊 Passage Reading I

Listen to the short passage for the first time. Then practise it by reading it aloud by yourself.

Huangguoshu Waterfall

Huangguoshu Waterfall is the largest waterfall in China, 78 meters high and 101 meters wide, which is located on the Baishui River of Guizhou Province. The rough and rapid water of the Baishui River rushes down directly from the cliffs to form a nine-stage waterfall. The falls send out a thunderous roar which can be heard from a long distance. When the sun shines over the waterfall, the mist appears changeably colorful through the refraction of the sun.

Huangguoshu Waterfall is listed in the national park of China. There are dozens of different falls, forming a picturesque view of karst landforms. The spectacular Grand Fall is the biggest in Asia. Its continuous flow of water varies in volume with the season.

Hidden behind the waterfall is the Water-Curtain Cave which traverses

Huangguoshu Waterfall. The total length of the cave is 134 meters, including six windows, five halls, and three springs. A road on the mountainside leads into the Water-Curtain Cave, where **the waterfall looks just like a huge curtain hanging in front of the cave**. Inside the cave, six windows let you view the falls from different angles; stretching your hand out of the window, you can touch the flying water. It looks like the Milky Way pouring down from the heaven. On a sunny day, a rainbow arches over the falls with misty clouds floating slowly over the valley. The Xiniu Pool, or the Rhinoceros Pool, 11 meters deep, is shaped like a rhinoceros. The waterfall pours into the pool with the force of a thousand horses galloping. Standing inside the Wangshui Pavilion, or the Water-Viewing Pavilion, beside the Rhinoceros Pool to enjoy the flow of the Huangguoshu Waterfall, **you may feel as if bunches of pearls and silver chains are falling upon you. What a grand and attractive scene!**

Task 4

Listen and Answer

You will hear five questions. Listen carefully and give an appropriate answer to each of them.

(1) _____

(2) _____

(3) _____

(4) _____

(5) _____

Task 5

Oral Practice

Please give a tour guide commentary on Huangguoshu Waterfall in your own words to your partner.

Item 8 Tour of Mountains

Model 4
West Lake 西湖

Task 1

Learning Points

Listen to the following *words, phrases,* and *useful expressions* and read along. Then try to memorize them.

🔊 **Words and Phrases**

causeway	n.	防堤
islet	n.	小岛
boast of		自豪地拥有，夸耀
the Outer Lake		外湖
the Inner Lake		里湖
the Yuehu Lake		岳湖
the West Inner Lake		西里湖
the Lesser South Lake		小南湖
the Solitary Hill		孤山
the Lesser Yingzhou		小瀛洲
the Mid-Lake Pavilion		湖心亭
the Islet of Lord Ruan		阮公墩
the Ten Scenic Spots of Qian-Tang		钱塘十景
the Eighteen Attractions of the West Lake		西湖十八景
Spring Dawn on the Su Causeway		苏堤春晓
Autumn Moon over the Calm Lake		平湖秋月
Three Pools Mirroring the Moon		三潭印月
Watching Goldfish in a Flowery Pond		花港观鱼
Snow Scene on the Broken Bridge		断桥残雪
Orioles Singing in the Willows		柳浪闻莺
Twin Peaks Piecing the Clouds		双峰插云

Evening Bell Ringing at the Nanping Hill	南屏晚钟
the Leifeng Pagoda in the Glow of the Setting Sun	雷峰夕照
Lotus in the Breeze at the Crooked Courtyard	曲院风荷
weeping willow	垂柳

Useful Expressions

1. Paradise in heaven, Suzhou and Hangzhou on earth.
   上有天堂，下有苏杭。
2. Thirty-six lakes though there are on the earth, the most famous one is in Hangzhou.
   天下西湖三十六，就中最好是杭州。
3. The four islands look like four glittering gems set in the rippling green waves, adding an unusual charm to the lake view.
   这四个小岛好像绿波荡漾中四枚闪闪发光的宝石，给西湖增添了非凡的魅力。
4. It is said that the lake looks more beautiful in the rain than in the sun, in the dark than in the rain, in the snow than in the dark.
   晴湖不如雨湖，雨湖不如夜湖，夜湖不如雪湖。

Task 2

Passage Reading II

Listen to the short passage for the first time. Then practise it by reading it aloud by yourself.

The West Lake

Hangzhou is well known for the beauty of the West Lake and the landscape around it. The saying, **"Paradise in heaven, Suzhou and Hangzhou on earth"**, is a fair reflection of people's admiration for this lovely city.

Su Dongpo, a literary master in the Song Dynasty, expressed his love for the West Lake in the following poem line, **"Thirty-six lakes though there are on the earth, the most famous one is in Hangzhou"**. In people's minds, the West Lake is a charming girl, simple and pure.

Lying in the west of the city and surrounded by hills on three sides, the West Lake is 3.2 kilometers from north to south and 2.8 kilometers from east to west. Two man-made causeways, namely the Su Causeway and the Bai Causeway, divide the lake into five separate water bodies: the Outer Lake, the Inner Lake, the Yuehu Lake, the West Inner Lake, and the Lesser South Lake. In the lake there are four islands: the Solitary Hill, the Lesser Yingzhou, the Mid-Lake Pavilion, and Ruan Gong Dun, or the Islet of Lord Ruan. **The four islands look like four glittering gems set in the rippling green waves, adding an unusual charm to the lake view.**

The West Lake boasts of its various beautiful scenic spots. Apart from "the Ten Scenic Spots of Qian-Tang" and "the Eighteen Attractions of the West Lake", the top ten famous scenic spots of the West Lake designated in the South Song Dynasty are as follows: Spring Dawn on the Su Causeway, Autumn Moon over the Calm Lake, Three Pools Mirroring the Moon, Watching Goldfish in a Flowery Pond, Snow Scene on the Broken Bridge, Orioles Singing in the Willows, Twin Peaks Piecing the Clouds, Evening Bell Ringing at the Nanping Hill, the Leifeng Pagoda in the Glow of the Setting Sun, and Lotus in the Breeze at the Crooked Courtyard.

Walking or cycling on the Su Causeway is a great fun. The weeping willows on either side of the causeway are pleasant to the eye. Standing on any of the six bridges, you can have a beautiful view of the lake, the hills, and pagodas. In fact, the West Lake offers charming views all year round. **It is said that the lake looks more beautiful in the rain than in the sun, in the dark than in the rain, in the snow than in the dark.**

Task 3

◀) Listen and Answer

You will hear five questions. Listen carefully and give an appropriate answer to each of them.

(1) _____

(2) _____

(3) _____

(4) _____

(5) _____

Task 4

Oral Practice

Retell the text in your own words.

Task 5

More Oral and Listening Practice:
【Listening】 Listen to the following passages and fill in the blanks.

Listening I

Touring Guilin

Guilin is primarily known for its charming and unique scenery. It has always been considered as _____. Many Chinese poets and painters, both _____, have been drawn to it, and they have all praised the beauty of Guilin _____.

Guilin offers tourists _____. Hills of Guilin are unique, which have been attracting _____ from all over the world _____. The hills have fantastically shaped peaks, studded with pines and small pavilions. So the landscape of Guilin has been praised as _____.

Listening II

Mount Lushan

Located in the northern part of Jiangxi Province, Mount Lushan faces the Yangtze River to the north and borders on the east with _____ in China, Poyang Lake. The mountain consists of _____, the tallest being Dahanyang, rising to the height of _____ above sea level. Altogether there are _____ in twelve scenic areas. The beauty of Lushan Mountain is attributed to its exotic peaks and mysterious caves, thunderous waterfalls, and gurgling springs, ancient temples and stone forest, and buildings that seem to be suspended in midair. With this fantastic blend of mountains, water, and cliffs, Mount Lushan is one of China's _____. Its beauty has been admired for centuries. About _____, Li Bai, a master poet of the Tang Dynasty, portrayed Mount Lushan in his poems, paying homage to the magnificent scenery he saw and enjoyed. He used this area as inspiration for many of his over _____. In 1996 Mount Lushan was listed as _____.

Item 8 Tour of Mountains

【Topics】Divide the class into groups. Choose one of the following topics to discuss in each group. Give a short report about the group's opinion after that.

1. What kind of personal requirements do you think a hotel receptionist should have?

2. Beijing is facing serious sandstorms, especially in spring and autumn. Do you regard it advisable to move our capital to another city?

3. Do you like to eat out or prepare dinner at home? Give your reasons according to the suggested points.

Eat out: avoid the boring processes of preparation and cleaning up; better flavor; variety of dishes; good environment; avoid quarrel or argument over chores involved with cooking and cleaning up.

Eat at home: less expensive; enhance relationship; sometimes romantic; more personal; enjoy cooking.

Item 9

☐☐☐☐

Tour of Temples 中国庙宇

- **Model 1**
  Visiting the Jade Buddha Temple 游览玉佛寺

- **Model 2**
  Visiting the Confucius Temple 孔子庙

- **Model 3**
  Visiting the Wudang Mountain 游览武当山

Model 1
Visiting the Jade Buddha Temple 游览玉佛寺

Task 1

Warm-up

Work in pairs. Discuss the following questions with your partner.

1. What are the main religions in China?
2. What are the Four Famous Buddhist Mountains in China? And where are they located respectively?
3. Have you heard of the Jade Buddha Temple in Shanghai? What is the temple most famous for?

Task 2

Learning Points

Listen to the following *words, phrases,* and *useful expressions* and read along. Then try to memorize them.

Words and Phrases

reign	n.	君主统治时期；任期；当政期
destruction	n.	毁灭；破坏
enshrine	v.	供奉
Myanmar	n.	缅甸
gold foils		金箔
meditation	n.	冥想；沉思
enlightenment	n.	启发；启迪
recumbent	adj.	横卧的
abbot	n.	方丈

Buddhist Master Huigen		慧根法师
Sakyamuni	*n.*	释迦牟尼
Maitreya	*n.*	弥勒菩萨
the Heavenly King Hall		天王殿
the Grand Hall		大雄宝殿
the Jade Buddha Tower		玉佛楼
cultural relics		文物
Dazang sutras		大藏经

🔊 Useful Expressions

1. I am interested in Buddhist temples.
   我对佛教寺庙感兴趣。
2. The two jade statues are of great artistic value and are regarded as treasures of Buddhism in our country.
   这两尊佛像具有极大的艺术价值，视为我国佛教珍品。
3. What kind of Buddha is enshrined and worshipped in this hall?
   这个大殿供奉哪位菩萨？
4. The Sitting Buddha is worshipped in the Jade Buddha Tower and the Recumbent Buddha is in the Recumbent Buddha Hall.
   坐佛供奉在玉佛楼，而卧佛供奉在卧佛殿。
5. The Sitting Buddha of Sakyamuni is 192 centimeters high and weighs 1000 kilograms.
   释迦牟尼的坐像高 1.92 米，重 1 吨。

Task 3

🔊 Dialogue I

Listen to *Dialogue I* for the first time. Then practise the dialogue by reading it aloud with your partner. Read through it at least twice, changing your role each time.

Visiting the Jade Buddha Temple

A: Miss Ding, a guide   B: Mr. Brown, an Australian tourist

A: Hi! Mr. Brown, we've arrived at our destination, the Jade Buddha Temple, a well-known Buddhist temple in Shanghai. Do you see the gate on the right?

B: What a beautiful gate! **I am interested in Buddhist temples**. When was the Jade Buddha Temple constructed?

A: The temple was constructed to house two jade Buddha statues in 1882, the eighth year of the reign of Guang Xu in the Qing Dynasty, and was rebuilt in 1918 after the destruction due to the war.

B: Two jade Buddha statues? Could you tell me more about the statues?

A: Sure. In 1882, Buddhist Master Huigen brought five jade Buddha statues to Shanghai from Myanmar. He had intended to ship the Buddha statues to the Putuo Mountain, however, due to the difficulty in transporting heavy Buddha statues, two jade statues of Sakyamuni were left in Shanghai.

B: That sounds interesting. They must be precious.

A: Yes, they are carved with whole white jade. **The two jade statues are of great artistic value and are regarded as treasures of Buddhism in our country.**

B: Great. The classical buildings in the temple seem attractive and unique. What is the tall building in front of us?

A: It is the Heavenly King Hall, one of the three major halls of the temple. The other two are the Grand Hall and the Jade Buddha Tower. Well, we have arrived at the Heavenly King Hall.

B: **What kind of Buddha is enshrined and worshipped in this hall?**

A: Maitreya, a laughing Buddha or the Cloth-bag Monk.

B: How about the Buddhas in the Grand Hall?

A: Three Buddhas with Sakyamuni in the middle.

B: Where are the two jade Buddhas worshipped?

A: **The Sitting Buddha is worshipped in the Jade Buddha Tower and the Recumbent Buddha is in the Recumbent Buddha Hall.** Let's go to the Jade Buddha Tower and visit the Sitting Buddha first.

B: All right.

A: Look. **The Sitting Buddha of Sakyamuni is 192 centimeters high and weights 1000 kilograms.** It is covered with gold foils and decorated with many precious stones, portraying the Buddha at the moment of his meditation and enlightenment.

B: Marvelous! The craft is perfect and unique. They are rare cultural relics.

A: Besides, more than 7,000 Dazang sutras are kept in the Jade Buddha Tower; these are all the invaluable cultural relics too.

B: I see. Let's go and visit the Recumbent Buddha.

A: Here we are. Look, the Recumbent Buddha is 96 centimeters long, lying on the right side with the right hand supporting the head and the left hand placed on the left leg. The serene face shows the peaceful mood of

Sakyamuni when he left this world.

B: Wonderful. What about the larger Recumbent Buddha?

A: Oh. This four-meter-long Recumbent Buddha was brought from Singapore by the tenth abbot of the temple in 1989.

B: Thank you very much for your excellent introduction.

A: It's my pleasure.

Task 4

Listen and Answer

You will hear five questions. Listen carefully and give an appropriate answer to each of them.

(1) _____

(2) _____

(3) _____

(4) _____

(5) _____

Task 5

Role-play

Act out the following dialogues.

【Situation A】 Miss Jiang is a tour guide who is taking a group of tourists around the Lingyin Temple in Hangzhou, a very famous Buddhist temple in China.

Miss Jiang:

☆ Says the Lingyin Temple is one of the most famous temples south of the Yangtze River.

☆ Tells that it is located at the foot of the Lingyin mountain, near the West Lake.

☆ Says the temple was founded in 328 AD, during the Eastern Jin Dynasty by Hui Li, an Indian monk.

☆ Says that the Lingyin Temple is mainly made up of the Hall of the Heavenly Kings（天王殿）, the Grand Hall of the Great Sage（大雄宝殿）, and the Hall of the Medicine Buddha（药师殿）.

☆ The plaque (匾) that is put on the front of the hall was written by the Kangxi Emperor of the Qing Dynasty, the major statue in this hall is that of the Maitreya Buddha, or the Laughing Buddha. At the back is the Skanda Buddha, or Weituo in Chinese. On the left and right are the Four Heavenly Kings.

☆ The Grand Hall is three-eaved and stands 33.6 metres tall. It houses a magnificent statue of Sakyamuni that stands 24.8 meters high. It is the largest wooden Buddhist statue in China, which was carved out of 24 pieces of camphor wood (香樟木).

☆ Behind the main hall is the Hall of the Medicine Buddha, housing a statue of the Medicine Buddha.

Tourists:

☆ Ask for the location of the Lingyin Temple.

☆ Want to know the story about the original construction of the temple.

☆ Ask for the temple's major halls.

☆ Ask questions when visiting the Hall of the Heavenly Kings: who wrote the plaque that is put on the front of the hall? What is the major statue of the hall? Who is the Buddha at the back of the Maitreya Buddha? Who are the Buddha statues on the both sides?

☆ Ask questions when visiting the Grand Hall of the Great Sage: ask for the information about a statue of Sakyamuni.

☆ Ask for information about the Hall of the Medicine Buddha.

【**Situation B**】 Miss Zhao, a tour guide, is taking the tourists around the Asoka Temple (阿育王寺) in Ningbo. Try to make a dialogue between the guide and the tourists according to the following clues.

☆ It is under the Luhua Peak in Taibai Mountains, 19 kilometers to the east of Ningbo.

☆ It was built in 282 AD, so it is more than 1700 years old.

☆ The temple covers 80,000 square meters.

☆ It is one of the China Five Buddhist Mountains, famous at home and abroad, and plays an important role in the exchange between China and Japan.

☆ It is famous for the Buddhist treasure: a bone from the top of Sakyamuni's head which is kept as a relic here.

☆ The Asoka Temple is grand in size with its splendid halls: the Grand Buddha Hall and the Hall of Stupa.

☆ On the Hall of Stupa hangs Emperor Song Gaozong's inscription "Foding Guangming Zhita" (Pagoda of Top Bright Buddha) and Emperor Song Xiao Zong "Miaosheng Zhidian" (The Most Wonderful Hall).

Item 9 Tour of Temples

Model 2
Visiting the Confucius Temple　游览孔子庙

Task 1

Warm-up

Work in pairs. Discuss the following questions with your partner.
1. What are your ideas about Confucius and Confucianism?
2. Have you been to Confucius' hometown of Qufu in Shandong Province? What is Qufu well-known for?

Task 2

Learning Points

Listen to the following *words, phrases,* and *useful expressions* and read along. Then try to memorize them.

🔊 **Words and Phrases**

itinerary	n.	旅程，行程
Confucius	n.	孔子
venerate	vt.	崇敬；敬重
sage	n.	圣人，智者
disciple	n.	弟子，门徒
scholar	n.	学者
prominent	adj.	卓越的，突出的
pillar	n.	柱子
Oriental Holy City		东方圣城
architectural complex		建筑群
an imperial tablet titled "Ode to Xingtan"		"杏坛赞"御碑

the Confucian temple	文庙
the Apricot Altar	杏坛
the Dacheng Palace	大成殿
the Thirteen-Monument Pavilion	十三碑亭
the Kuiwen Tower	奎文阁

🔊 Useful Expressions

1. We are on our tour of Qufu, the hometown of Confucius and an "Oriental Holy City".
   我们赴孔子故里，有"东方圣城"之称的曲阜旅游。

2. You will be seeing the largest Confucian temple in the world and one of the largest ancient architectural complexes in China.
   你们将看到世界上最大的文庙，它是中国最大的古建筑群之一。

3. They are the Dacheng Palace, the Apricot Altar, the Thirteen-Monument Pavilion, and the Kuiwen Tower.
   孔庙的主要景点有大成殿、杏坛、十三碑亭和奎文阁。

4. The Dacheng Palace is the highest building in the temple and one of the three major ancient palaces in China.
   大成殿是孔庙的最高建筑，也是中国三大古殿之一。

5. The Apricot Altar is the place where Confucius gave his lectures in his later years.
   杏坛为孔子晚年讲学之处。

6. Yes, it was said that he had 3,000 students in all his life and 72 of them were more prominent.
   是的，据传孔子有"弟子三千，贤人七十二"。

7. In the Apricot Altar, there is also an imperial tablet titled "Ode to Xingtan" written by Emperor Qianlong in the Qing Dynasty.
   杏坛里还有清朝乾隆皇帝所写的"杏坛赞"御碑。

Task 3

🔊 Dialogue III

Listen to *Dialogue III* for the first time. Then practise the dialogue by reading it aloud with your partner. Read through it at least twice, changing your role each time.

Item 9 Tour of Temples

Visiting the Temple of Confucius

A: Lily, a tour guide   B: tourists from England

A: Good morning, ladies and gentlemen. I am your tour guide and my English name is Lily. **We are on our tour of Qufu, the hometown of Confucius and an " Oriental Holy City ".**

B: That sounds interesting. Lily, would you please introduce today's itinerary?

A: All right. Today we will visit the three attractions concerning Confucius one after another: The Temple of Confucius, the Mansion of Confucius, and the Forest of Confucius. Our first stop will be The Temple of Confucius.

B: Thanks a lot.

A: Here we are. The Temple of Confucius is on your right. **You will be seeing the largest Confucian temple in the world and one of the largest ancient architectural complexes in China.**

B: The Temple of Confucius is grand and magnificent. When and for what purpose was the temple built?

A: In 478 B.C., the year after Confucius' death, the king of the State of Lu transformed Confucius' former residence into a temple to venerate the sage. However, for centuries emperors ordered that his disciples and other famous persons be venerated here, too. Now the list is up to 172 scholars.

B: Yeah, what are the main attractions of the Temple of Confucius?

A: **They are the Dacheng Palace, the Apricot Altar, the Thirteen-Monument Pavilion, and the Kuiwen Tower.**

B: What is this splendid building, Lily?

A: It is the Dacheng Palace, the core palace of the Temple of Confucius. The palace is 24.8 meters high, 45.69 meters long, and 24.85 meters wide. **It is the highest building in the temple and one of the three major ancient palaces in China.**

B: Are the three golden Chinese characters for "Dacheng Palace"?

A: Yes, you are right. They are written by Emperor Yongzheng in the Qing Dynasty. Have you noticed the 28 stone pillars carved with dragons? Each pillar has nine dragons and the pillars are about 500 years old.

B: That's pretty old.

A: Ladies and gentlemen, here is the Apricot Altar. **This is the place where Confucius gave his lectures in his later years.**

B: Confucius had a lot of students, didn't he?

A: **Yes, it was said that he had 3,000 students in all his life and 72 of them were more prominent.**

B: He deserves the title of a great educator.

A: **In the Apricot Altar, there is also an imperial tablet titled "Ode to Xingtan" written by Emperor Qianlong in the Qing Dynasty.** The ancient tree beside it is said to be planted by Confucius himself.

B: Thanks a lot for your commentaries.

A: You are welcome.

Task 4

Listen and Answer

You will hear five questions. Listen carefully and give an appropriate answer to each of them.

(1) _____

(2) _____

(3) _____

(4) _____

(5) _____

Task 5

Role-play

Act out the following dialogues.

【Situation A】 Lily is a tour guide who is going to take a group of tourists around the Mansion of Confucius in Qufu.

Tourists:

☆ Ask for the location of the Mansion of Confucius.

☆ Ask for the area of the mansion and basic knowledge about the mansion.

☆ Ask whether Confucius lived in this mansion.

☆ Ask for the meaning of "Lord Yansheng" （衍圣公）.

☆ Ask for the information about the Grand Hall （大堂）.

Lily:

☆ Says it's in the east of the Temple of Confucius.

☆ Says that the mansion covers 240 mu (about 16 hectares), and it has nine courtyards with 480 rooms, and houses can be divided into two parts: offices in the front and residences behind it.

☆ Tells that this is the living quarters for Confucius' descendants and it was also referred to as Lord Yansheng's residence.

☆ Answers the concrete meaning: it means the Duke of Yansheng, a title given to the descendants of Confucius by the emperor in the Song Dynasty. It is a hereditary title. In the Ming Dynasty, an independent Residence of Lord Yansheng was set up, the yamen（衙门） in the front and the domestic household at the back.

☆ Tells that the Grand Hall as a public court of Lord Yansheng is featured by tiger-skin chairs, a giant seal, the four necessities in the study, etc.

【Situation B】 Lily is a tour guide who continues to take a group of tourists around the Forest of Confucius in Qufu. Make up a dialogue between the guide and tourists in accordance with the clues given.

Tourists:

☆ Ask for the location of the Forest of Confucius.

☆ Ask what they can see in the Forest of Confucius.

☆ Ask whether Confucius' tomb is situated in the forest.

☆ Ask for the area of the Forest of Confucius.

☆ Ask whether there are a variety of trees in the forest.

☆ Say the forest is like a botanic garden.

☆ Say the forest is too big and ask whether they should explore it on foot.

☆ Ask whether there are some other famous persons' tombs.

Lily:

☆ Tells that it is located in the northern Qufu, about two kilometers from the city center.

☆ Says that the forest is the Confucius Family Cemetery, it has been the historic burial ground of the Confucius family for more than 2,000 years and members of the family are still buried there today.

☆ Answers the question: Confucius' tomb is in the center of the forest. After Confucius died in 479 B.C., he was buried here. His descendants were buried at the same place. The place gradually grew into a cemetery with over 100,000 tombs and 4,000 steles.

☆ Tells that the Forest of Confucius covers an area of two square kilometers and it has become the largest family cemetery in the world.

☆ Tells that since Zigong planted the first tree for Confucius, planting strange trees in the forest has historically been viewed as an act of veneration and now there are over 10,000 trees in the forest.

☆ Tells the cemetery is in fact a forest and it is a good place to get relief from the hustle and bustle of the city.

☆ Says "no" and they can rent a bike just inside the entrance.

☆ Tells that Kong Shangren, the famous author of the "Peach Blossom Fan" was buried here too.

Model 3
Visiting the Wudang Mountain 游览武当山

Task 1

Learning Points

Listen to the following *words, phrases,* and *useful expressions* and read along. Then try to memorize them.

🔊 **Words and Phrases**

cluster	v.	使……集中，簇拥
numerous	adj.	许多，很多
exotic	adj.	奇异的，异国他乡的
homage	n.	崇敬，致敬
miracle	n.	奇迹
represent	vt.	代表，象征
exquisite	adj.	精致的，精美的
advocate	vt.	提倡，主张
gold-gilded	adj.	镀金的
foster	vt.	培养，养育
fossil	n.	化石
the Five Dragon Ancestral Temple		五龙宫
the Tianzhu Peak		天柱峰
the Golden Hall		金殿
the Taihe Temple		太和宫
the Southern Crag Palace		南岩宫
the Purple Cloud Palace		紫霄宫
the Yuzhen Temple		遇真宫
Wudang boxing		武当拳
Zhang Sanfeng		张三丰

Item 9 Tour of Temples

🔊 Useful Expressions

1. Clustering around the Tianzhu Peak are numerous outstanding peaks and exotic sceneries as if "ten thousand peaks are paying their homage".
   众多奇峰异景环绕天柱峰，形成"万山朝大顶"的奇观。

2. The large architectural complex includes nine palaces, nine monasteries, 72 cliff temples, 36 nunneries, 39 bridges, and 12 pavilions with a total floor space of 1.6 million square meters.
   宏大建筑群包括九宫、九观、岩庙、三十六庵堂、三十九桥、十二亭，总建筑面积达 160 万平方米。

3. In December 1994, the ancient building complex of the Wudang Mountain was listed as the World Cultural Heritage.
   1994 年 12 月，武当山古建筑群被列为世界文化遗产。

4. A ten-ton sitting statue of God Zhenwu in the hall is an exquisite example of ancient Chinese art of copper casting.
   金殿内重达十吨的真武大帝坐像是我国古代铜铸艺术的精品。

5. The Daoist music in the mountain is also a living fossil of the music of China.
   武当山的道教音乐也是中华音乐的活化石。

Task 2

🔊 Passage Reading

Listen to the short passage for the first time. Then practise it by reading it aloud by yourself.

The Wudang Mountain

The Wudang Mountain is situated in Danjiangkou city in Hubei Province. Its main peak, the Tianzhu Peak, is 1,612 meters above the sea level. **Clustering around the Tianzhu Peak are numerous outstanding peaks and exotic sceneries as if "ten thousand peaks are paying their homage".** The mountain's scenic spots mainly include 72 peaks, 36 rocky cliffs, 24 streams, three pools, nine wells, and ten lakes.

As a treasure house of the nation, the Wudang Mountain is renowned for its magnificent and grand Daoist palaces, which are miracles of the world ancient architecture. The oldest temple on the Wudang Mountain is the Five Dragon Ancestral Temple which dates back to the 7th century AD. Most of the ancient buildings on the mountain were built in the Ming Dynasty. Being a Daoist, Emperor Zhu Di of the Ming Dynasty ordered 300,000 people to start construction in the Mountain for 12 years. The Golden Hall, the Taihe Temple, the Southern Crag Palace, the Purple Cloud Palace, and the Yuzhen Temple were all built during this time. **The large architectural complex includes nine palaces, nine monasteries, 72 cliff temples, 36 nunneries, 39 bridges, and 12 pavilions with a total floor space of 1.6 million square meters.** The palaces and temples in the Wudang Mountain represent higher standards of Chinese art and architecture during a period of nearly 1,000 years. **In December 1994, the ancient building complex of the Wudang Mountain was listed as the World Cultural Heritage.**

The Golden Hall on the main peak is a copper wonder. Built in 1416 AD, the gold-gilded hall is 5.5 meters high, 4.4 meters wide, and 3.15 meters deep and is completely copper-cast, except for its base. **A ten-ton sitting statue of God Zhenwu in the hall is an exquisite example of ancient Chinese art of copper casting.**

The Wudang Mountain is the source of the Wudang boxing (Tai Chi) created by Zhang Sanfeng. Wudang boxing advocates the cultivation of morality and fostering of nature. **The Daoist music in the mountain is also a living fossil of the music of China.**

Task 3

🔊 Listen and Answer

You will hear five questions. Listen carefully and give an appropriate answer to each of them.

(1) _____

(2) _____

(3) _____

(4) _____

(5) _____

Task 4

Oral Practice

Retell the text in your own words.

Item 9 Tour of Temples

Task 5

More Oral and Listening Practice:

【Listening】 Listen to the dialogues and fill in the blanks.

🔊 Listening I

Visiting the Jinshan Temple

A: Ladies and gentlemen, now we are at the main entrance to the Jinshan Temple.

B: _____?

A: Yes, that is true.

B: _____.

A: Sure. It is made up of several halls. Now let's walk into the forecourt through this gate. _____.

B: Why are so many tourists standing in line before the bell tower?

A: They are waiting for their turns to strike the bell, _____ _____. And bell-striking is one of the oldest Chinese traditions.

B: It seems the bell is made of bronze. _____?

A: It is centuries old. Please look at the four figures in front of you.

B: _____? They frightened me.

A: They are four guardian warriors.

B: I see. _____.

A: Exactly. Well, we are now in the Grand Hall. _____ _____. It is always smiling.

B: Yeah, who is it?

A: It's Maitreya Buddha, also called the laughing monk.

🔊 Listening II

Visiting Leshan Giant Buddha of Sichuan

A: Ladies and gentlemen, we've arrived at the tourist site of Leshan Giant Buddha. _____.

B: What a magnificent Buddha! From this angle I could hardly see his head. The Buddha looks like a hill.

A: Yes, it is. _____. There goes a saying, "The hill is a Buddha and the Buddha is a hill." It is the biggest Maitreya Buddha in the world.

B: _____. How was it chiseled (凿出) out of the mountain?

A: It was very hard to chisel Leshan Giant Buddha from the mountain. It was recorded that _____ to complete the huge project.

B: Look, what are those on the Buddha's head? They look like stone balls.

A: They are hair curls of the Giant Buddha. _____.

B: Amazing! Look at his ears. They are so big.

A: Right. Each of his ears is seven meters long. _____. Look down at his feet. Over 100 men can sit down on each of its 8.5-meter-wide insteps.

B: _____. It's a marvel of the stone sculptures in the world.

A: Now we have reached the feet of the Giant Buddha. Look up at the Buddha!

B: Oh, we are all dwarfs (矮子) compared with the Buddha.

A: Now you can take pictures in front of it. _____. Have fun!

B: Thanks!

【Topics】Divide the class into groups. Choose one of the following topics to discuss in each group. Give a short report about the group's opinion after that.

1. Brief introduction to the main religions in China and their respective emphases on religious doctrines.

2. Name the Four Famous Buddhist Mountains in China and give an English tour commentary about one of them.

3. List the Four Famous Daoist Mountains in China and offer an English tour commentary about one of them.

Item 10

Tours of Historical Sites
名胜古迹之旅

- **Model 1**
  A Tour of the Forbidden City   游览紫禁城

- **Model 2**
  The Tour of the Great Wall   长城之旅

- **Model 3**
  The Tianyi Pavilion Library   天一阁藏书楼

Model 1
A Tour of the Forbidden City 游览紫禁城

Task 1

Warm-up

Work in pairs. Try to answer the questions below.
1. Why is the Palace Museum also called the Forbidden City?
2. Could you name the three main halls in the front part of the Forbidden City?

Task 2

Learning Points

Listen to the following *words, phrases,* and *useful expressions* and read along. Then try to memorize them.

🔊 Words and Phrases

anxious	*adj.*	焦急的，忧虑的
imperial	*adj.*	帝国的
gorgeous	*adj.*	极好的
elaborate	*adj.*	复杂的
exquisite	*adj.*	精巧的
carving	*n.*	雕刻品
terrace	*n.*	台阶
marble	*n.*	大理石
crown	*n*	皇冠，王冠
	v	为……加冕；形成……顶部
edict	*n.*	布告
feudal	*adj.*	封建的

Item 10 Tours of Historical Sites

The Forbidden City	紫禁城
The Palace Museum	故宫
royal court	宫廷
The Hall of Supreme Harmony	太和殿
The Hall of Central Harmony	中和殿
The Hall of Preserving Harmony	保和殿

🔊 Useful Expressions

1. This is the world-famous Forbidden City where once emperors, empresses and their families lived.
   这就是世界著名的紫禁城，皇帝、皇后和他们的家人曾经居住于此。
2. It was formerly used on such occasions as a new emperor's crowning, the emperor's birthday, and the announcement of important edicts.
   太和殿以前是举行皇帝加冕仪式、皇帝做寿和宣布重要事件的地方。
3. It was here that the feudal emperors handled their daily affairs.
   中和殿是皇帝用来处理日常事务的地方。
4. Banquets and royal examinations were held here.
   那里（保和殿）是用来举办宴会和殿试的地方。

Task 3

🔊 Dialogue I

Listen to *Dialogue I* for the first time. Then practise the dialogue by reading it aloud with your partner. Read through it at least twice, changing your role each time.

A Tour of the Forbidden City

A: the local guide   B: the tourists

A: Good morning everyone. Now, we're going to visit the Palace Museum. Have you ever heard of it?

B1: Yes, but I only have a little knowledge of it. I'm anxious to have a sightseeing tour there.

B2: Everything is OK. Now, let's set off.

A: (An hour later) Now we are standing on the grounds of the imperial palace.

B3: Oh! It is so gorgeous and elaborate, indeed.

A: **This is the world-famous Forbidden City where once emperors, empresses, and their families lived.**

B4: Yes, I can feel the grandness.

A: Let's move on.

B1: What exquisite carvings! What's that white terrace?

A: That's the marble terrace on which the three main halls of the front part of the palace were built.

B2: I'm eager to see.

A: Attention, please. This is the Hall of Supreme Harmony. **It was formerly used on such occasions as a new emperor's crowning, the emperor's birthday, and the announcement of important edicts.**

B3: This hall is quite different from any of the royal courts I have seen in the west.

A: Yes, it is. Go ahead.

B4: Shall we proceed to the next hall?

A: Yes. Let's go on. This is the Hall of Central Harmony. **It was here that the feudal emperors handled their daily affairs.**

B2: How splendid! The atmosphere here is so peaceful and tranquil.

A: The last of the three is the Hall of Preserving Harmony. It was built in the Ming Dynasty. **Banquets and royal examinations were held here.**

B1: Thank you for your excellent explanation. I learned a lot about China.

A: It's my real pleasure.

Task 4

🔊 Listen and Answer

You will hear five questions. Listen carefully and give an appropriate answer to each of them.

(1) _____

(2) _____

(3) _____

(4) _____

(5) _____

Item 10 Tours of Historical Sites

Task 5

Role-play

Act out the following dialogues.

【Situation A】 Mr. Tang is a tour guide who is showing a team of tourists from the USA around the Forbidden City.

Mr. Tang:
☆ Greets the tourists.
☆ Introduces the history of the Forbidden City.
☆ Explains the marble terrace.
☆ Explains the three main halls.

Tourists:
☆ Want to know the history of the Forbidden City.
☆ Appreciate the grand scenes and want to know something about the white terrace.
☆ Express eagerness to see the three main halls of the front part of the palace.
☆ Give exciting remarks.

【Situation B】 Mr. Jones, a friend of Tian Jun, comes to Xi'an. Tian and Mr. Jones go to visit the Terracotta Warriors. Tian was born and brought up in Xi'an and acts as a tour guide for Mr. Jones.

Model 2
The Tour of the Great Wall 长城之旅

Task 1

Warm-up

Work in pairs. Try to answer the questions below.
1. Do you know the Eight Great Wonders in the world?
2. Can you tell the story of "Mengjiangnv Weeping on the Great Wall" to your partner?

Task 2

Learning Points

Listen to the following *words, phrases,* and *useful expressions* and read along. Then try to memorize them.

🔊 Words and Phrases

ascend	v.	上升，攀登
construction	n.	建设，建造
collapsed	adj.	倒塌的
existing	adj.	现有的
crystallization	n.	结晶
wisdom	n.	智慧
photograph	n.	相片
beacon-fire tower		烽火台
invasion	n.	侵入，侵略
nomadic	adj.	游牧民族的
tribe	n.	部落
breathtaking	adj.	吃惊的

| challenge | n./v. | 挑战 / 向……挑战 |
| top | n. | 极点，最高地位 |

🔊 Useful Expressions

1. The construction of the Great wall started in the 7th century B.C. during the Zhou Dynasty and continued until the Qing Dynasty in the 17th century.
   长城的建造从公元前 7 世纪的周朝开始，一直延续到 17 世纪的清朝。
2. The Great Wall is indeed the crystallization of the industry and wisdom of the Chinese people, and also a symbol of ancient Chinese culture.
   长城是中国人民勤奋和智慧的结晶，也是中国古代文化的象征。
3. The Great Wall was built to guard against invasion by nomadic tribes from the north.
   建造长城是用来抵御北方游牧部落的侵略。
4. Some people have walked from Shanhaiguan all the way to Jiayuguan.
   有一些人从山海关一直走到嘉峪关。
5. Each of the two ends of the Great Wall is called a "guan".
   长城的两个尽头均称为"关"。

Task 3

🔊 Dialogue II

Listen to *Dialogue II* for the first time. Then practise the dialogue by reading it aloud with your partner. Read through it at least twice, changing your role each time.

The Tour of the Great Wall

G: the guide   T: the tourist

G: There is a famous saying: " A man who has never been to the Great Wall is not a true man". Now we're going to ascend the Great Wall. Are you ready?

T: Yes, of course.

G: Have you heard of the story of Meng Jiangnv?

T: It has something to do with the Great wall, doesn't it?

G: Quite right.

T: Would you please tell us the story of it? We'd like very much to hear the whole story.

G: Sure. In the construction of the Great Wall many laborers lost their lives.

Meng Jiangnv came to the Great wall with clothes for her husband only to find that he had died. She was heartbroken and wept so bitterly that part of the Wall collapsed. When she found her husband's body lying under the wall, she threw herself into the sea.

T: What a faithful wife. And would you tell us more details about the famous Wall?

G: OK. **The construction of the Great wall started in the 7th century B.C. during the Zhou Dynasty and continued until the Qing Dynasty in the 17th century,** taking altogether more than 2,000 years.

T: **The Great Wall is indeed the crystallization of the industry and wisdom of the Chinese people, and also a symbol of ancient Chinese culture.** How long is the Great Wall? It is said you can even see it from the moon.

G: The total length of the Great Wall is about 21196 kilometers.

T: It is beautiful, even better than the Great Wall I've seen in photographs. What are the towers on the wall?

G: Oh, they are called beacon-fire towers. You know, **the Great Wall was built to guard against invasion by nomadic tribes from the north.** When people found the enemy approaching, they would send smoke signals from the tower as a warning. When other guards in the nearby tower saw the signals, they would do the same. In this way, the signals would be sent all the way to the capital.

T: How clever the ancient people were!

G: Come on! Let's keep climbing up, the scene's even more breathtaking up there.

T: Has anyone ever walked to the end of the Great Wall?

G: Sure, **some people have walked from Shanhaiguan all the way to Jiayuguan.**

T: Really? That might be a challenge. What is a "guan"?

G: **Each of the two ends of the Great Wall is called a "guan".** Look, there are even people up there. Come on, let's have a race to see who can get to the top first!

T: OK, let's go!

Task 4

🔊 Listen and Answer

You will hear five questions. Listen carefully and give an appropriate answer to each of them.

(1) _____

(2) _____

(3) _____

(4) _____

(5) _____

Task 5

Role-play

Act out the following dialogues.

【Situation A】 Xiao Zhao, a tour guide, takes a group of foreign tourists to the Great Wall. The tourists asks some questions about the famous wall and Xiao Zhao answers these questions.

Xiao Zhao:
☆ Greets the tourists.
☆ Introduces the story of Meng Jiangnv.
☆ Introduces the time of the construction of the Great Wall.
☆ Tells that it is about 21,196 kilometers long.
☆ Tells that they are beacon-fire towers and their function.
☆ Explains the meaning of "guan".

Tourists:
☆ Greet the guide.
☆ Want to know the story of Meng Jiangnv.
☆ Want to know the time of its construction.
☆ Ask how long the Great Wall is.
☆ Ask what the towers are on the wall.
☆ Ask the meaning of "guan".

【Situation B】 The local guide is showing Mr. Davis around the Temple of Heaven. Mr. Davis is eager to know some information about the imperial temple and the guide tries their best to satisfy him.

Model 3
The Tianyi Pavilion Library 天一阁藏书楼

Task 1

Learning Points

Listen to the following *words, phrases,* and *useful expressions* and read along. Then try to memorize them.

🔊 Words and Phrases

pavilion	n.	楼阁
equivalent	adj.	等价的，相等的
combination	n.	结合，联合
collect	v.	聚集
posterity	n.	后代
abide	v.	遵守
aggressor	n.	侵略者
missionary	n.	传教士
chronicle	n.	年代记，记录，编年史
architecture	n.	建筑学，建筑业
elegant	adj.	优雅的，精美的
flush	adj.	丰足的，齐平的
gable	n.	山墙，三角墙
corridor	n.	走廊
rockery	n.	（为种植高山植物而造的）假山庭园
kiosk	n.	亭
national defense minister		国防部部长

🔊 Useful Expressions

1. The Tianyi Pavilion Library is the oldest well-preserved private library in China

today.

天一阁是中国现存最古老的、保存较为完好的私人藏书楼。

2. Never discard the books, and never take the books away.

代不分书，书不出阁。

3. They are rich sources of local chronicles and imperial examinations and are precious materials for the study of history, people, social customs, and habits.

这些书主要是（明朝的）地方志和科举录，是研究历史、民情、社会习俗的珍贵资料。

4. It is not only world famous for its wide collection of books, but also for its unique architecture and elegant landscape.

天一阁不仅以其博大的藏书著称于世，而且以其独特的建筑风格和优雅的环境而闻名。

Task 2

🔊 Passage Reading

Listen to the short passage for the first time. Then practise it by reading it aloud by yourself.

The Tianyi Pavilion Library

  The Tianyi Pavilion is located in the west of Yuehu Lake in Ningbo City, Zhejiang Province. It was built by Fan Qin, a high-ranking official equivalent to today's national defense minister, during Emperor Jia Jing's reign in the Ming Dynasty (1368—1644). **The Tianyi Pavilion Library is the oldest well-preserved private library in China today.** It is a combination of culture, social studies, history, and art.

  Fan Qin loved collecting ancient books all his life, and his collection of books reached 70,000. To protect the books, Fan Qin made strict family rules that all the posterity should abide by the teachings of the deceased: **Never discard the books, and never take the books away.** However, many books disappeared as the years passed by. In the thirteenth year (1808) of the Jiaqing reign of the Qing Dynasty, books in the pavilion totaled to 4,049 in more than 53,000 volumes. During the Opium War, British aggressors plundered many books and sold them to French missionaries and paper mills. After many accidents, books in the pavilion merely totaled 1,591 in 13,038 volumes in 1940. After the founding of the People's Republic of China, special management departments were set up to protect the Tianyi Pavilion. More than

3,000 volumes of missing books were found.

Now, the Tianyi Pavilion keeps a large collection of about 300,000 ancient books, among which 80,000 are rare copies including the woodcut copies and handwritten copies of the Song and Ming Dynasties. **They are rich sources of local chronicles and imperial examinations and are precious materials for the study of history, people, social customs, and habits.**

The Tianyi Pavilion Library is called the "Book City of South China". **It is not only world famous for its wide collection of books, but also for its unique architecture and elegant landscape.**

The Tianyi Pavilion has a flush gable roof, and is six bays wide and deep, with a corridor extending from the front to the back. In front of the pavilion is a pond that stores water for fireproofing. Fan Wenguang, Fan Qin's great-grandson, rebuilt the pavilion by laying rockery around the lake, building kiosks and bridges, planting flowers and grass in the fourth year (1665) of the Kangxi reign in the Qing Dynasty.

Task 3

🔊 Listen and Answer

You will hear five questions. Listen carefully and give an appropriate answer to each of them.

(1) _____

(2) _____

(3) _____

(4) _____

(5) _____

Task 4

Oral Practice

Retell the text in your own words.

Item 10 Tours of Historical Sites

Task 5

More Oral and Listening Practice:
【Listening】 Listen to the following dialogue and passage and fill in the blanks.

🔊 Listening I

Visiting Mogao Grottos

T: My goodness, the Mogao Grottos have five stories.
G: _____.
T: Amazing! Some stand alone, and others are together. All are arranged in ___ _____.
G: In the Yungang Grottos and the Longmen Grottos, statues are carved out of rock, but here they are sculpted out of clay.
T: _____?
G: A local plant from the desert here was used to wrap the _____, and then clay was used for sculpture.
T: _____.
G: Because the statues were painted. It's called painted sculpture.
T: Those _____ were really smart.
G: There is a _____ of murals in the Mogao Grottos, too. People believe there may be as many as 45,000 _____ of them. If they were put end to end, they would _____ a two-meter-high, 25-kilometer-long art gallery.
T: Wow, that's _____.

🔊 Listening II

Lao She Teahouse

Lao She Teahouse, established in _____, is named for the _____ _____, Lao She, and one of his better-known works, "Teahouse". At the teahouse, customers sit in _____, drink the best teas in China, watch all kinds of _____, and enjoy delicious traditional Beijing _____ which were eaten by Qing Dynasty emperors. Since its opening, Lao She Teahouse has _____ many famous people from China and all over the world; _____, the Teahouse is well-known in _____. In 1994, former United States

President, George Bush visited the teahouse. Other _____ include former _____ Kurt Waldheim and the Singaporean President, Wang Dingchang.

【Topics】Divide the class into groups. Choose one of the following topics to discuss in each group. Give a short report about the group's opinion after that.

1. Can you list the characteristics of Chinese tourism? (It may contain the scenic spots, the service, the unique products, etc.)
2. Why do you think young people in cities like to hang out in bars?
3. Why does China enjoy a worldwide reputation for its cooking?

Item 11

◻◻◻◻

Tour of Chinese Characteristic Culture
中国特色文化之旅

- **Model 1**
  Tai Chi   太极拳

- **Model 2**
  Spring Festival   春节

- **Model 3**
  Peking Opera   京剧

- **Model 4**
  China-Home of Tea   茶乡中国

Model 1
Tai Chi 太极拳

Task 1

Warm-up

Work in pairs. Learn the following words of Chinese traditional sports and games. Then answer the questions below.

wrestling	horsemanship	archery	kicking the shuttlecock
dragon boat racing	kite-flying	martial arts	

1. Do you like sports and games? Why?
2. Which one is your favorite? Why?

Task 2

Learning Points

Listen to the following *words, phrases,* and *useful expressions* and read along. Then try to memorize them.

🔊 Words and Phrases

superior	*adj.*	上好的
internal	*adj.*	内部的
circular	*adj.*	循环的
coordinate	*v.*	协调
martial arts		武术（指功夫、柔道、空手道等）
in terms of		在……方面
concentrate on		全神贯注于，专注于

be superior to   优于

🔊 Useful Expressions

1. Tai Chi refers to the philosophic idea of the universe.
   太极拳体现了哲学的宇宙论。
2. Tai Chi features gentle and circular movements.
   太极拳以动作柔和与循环为特征。
3. Tai Chi is a sport that strengthens the body as well as the mind from within.
   太极拳是一项强健身心的运动。
4. The most basic principles are focusing on breathing control and the coordinated body movements.
   （太极拳）最基本的原理是注重呼吸的控制和身体动作的协调。
5. I'd be glad to.
   我愿意。

Task 3

🔊 Dialogue I

Listen to *Dialogue I* for the first time. Then practise the dialogue by reading it aloud with your partner. Read through it at least twice, changing your role each time.

Tai Chi

G: the guide   T: the tourist

T: What does Tai Chi mean? Is it superior to other martial arts?

G: Not exactly. **Tai Chi refers to the philosophic idea of the universe.** It is the continuous cycle of life.

T: How does it differ from other martial arts?

G: In terms of movements, **Tai Chi features gentle and circular movements.** It is especially different from many western types of sports in which the harder and the quicker, the better.

T: How could you benefit from such a relaxed way?

G: **Tai Chi is a sport that strengthens the body as well as the mind from within.** It provides the mental relaxation. And it is known in China for centuries to be effective for some internal diseases.

T: That's why it is so popular, I should say. Is it easy to learn?
G: Yes. It is easy to learn for health improvement.
T: What are the essentials for practicing Tai Chi?
G: **The most basic principles are focusing on breathing control and the coordinated body movements.**
T: Would you please show us how to do it?
G: **I'd be glad to**. Now follow me. You can also have a try.

Task 4

🔊 Listen and Answer

You will hear five questions. Listen carefully and give an appropriate answer to each of them.

1. _____
2. _____
3. _____
4. _____
5. _____

Task 5

Role-play

Act out the following dialogues.

【Situation A】 Yao Tian and his foreign friend John are doing morning exercise in the Moon Lake Park. They find that a lot of people are doing martial arts. John feels it interesting, so he is asking Yao Tian some questions about Wushu.

John:
☆ Finds that a lot of people are doing martial arts.
☆ Asks why Chinese people like it.
☆ Asks what martial arts means and its history.
☆ Hopes to learn it.

Yao Tian:
☆ Tells John that Chinese people are fond of martial arts.

Item 11 Tour of Chinese Characteristic Culture

☆ Answers that people take up martial arts for physical training and self-defense.

☆ Says that martial arts are practiced in various types of set exercises, either empty-handed or with weapons, with its history dating back several thousand years.

☆ Feels glad to teach John.

【Situation B】 Talk with your partner about some traditional Chinese games that are played by Chinese children and adults respectively.

【Situation C】 Discuss with your partner about traditional Chinese sports that are played by the Han people and people of national minorities.

Model 2
Spring Festival 春节

Task 1

Warm-up

Work in pairs. Think about the following question and discuss with your partner.
What festivals are popular in our country? How do we spend these festivals?

Task 2

Learning Points

Listen to the following *words, phrases,* and *useful expressions* and read along. Then try to memorize them.

🔊 Words and Phrases

terrific	*adj.*	极好的
firework	*n.*	焰火
firecracker	*n.*	爆竹，鞭炮
dispel	*v.*	驱散，驱逐
cuisine	*n.*	烹饪
speciality	*n.*	专长，擅长
dish	*n.*	一道菜肴
feast	*n.*	宴会，酒席
chopstick	*n.*	[复数] 筷子
considerate	*adj.*	考虑周到的
prime	*n.*	全盛时期
essential	*adj.*	必要的，本质的
Ningbo Municipal Government		宁波市政府

Item 11 Tour of Chinese Characteristic Culture

feast one's eyes on	尽情欣赏（艺术品）
work of art	艺术品
take pictures of	拍照
remind sb. of sth.	提醒（某人）（某事）
to tell one's truth	说实话
the Spring Festival Gala	春节联欢晚会
stay up	熬夜

🔊 Useful Expressions

1. How did you spend the Spring Festival in China?
   你在中国怎么过的春节？
2. It is believed that …
   据说……
3. I really feasted my eyes on the Chinese food.
   中国菜肴让我一饱眼福。
4. I couldn't have the heart to eat it.
   我不忍心吃。
5. Thank you for saying so.
   谢谢您这么说。

Task 3

🔊 Dialogue II

Listen to *Dialogue II* for the first time. Then practise the dialogue by reading it aloud with your partner. Read through it at least twice, changing your role each time.

Spring Festival

H: Helen (a Chinese student)   B: Philips Bush (an American professor)

H: Happy New Year! Professor Bush, **how did you spend the Spring Festival in China?**

B: Oh, it was terrific. I was excited when I saw beautiful fireworks in the evening sky on New Year's Eve. I was simply amazed.

H: That's a typical Chinese traditional custom. **It is believed that** firecrackers and fireworks will be able to dispel bad luck and bring good fortune in the coming year. By the way, where did you have your Nianyefan, Professor Bush?

B: Oh, I was invited to a dinner party given by Ningbo Municipal Government. **I really feasted my eyes on the Chinese food.**

H: Really? In China, we have eight major cuisines, such as Beijing food, Shandong food, Cantonese food, etc., and in each cuisine, there are some specialties.

B: That's right. In my eyes, each dish was a work of art. It was so beautiful that **I couldn't have the heart to eat it,** so I took pictures of the dishes, which would surely remind me of the wonderful feast.

H: That's a good idea. But as I know, you can't use chopsticks well, how did you enjoy yourself at the dinner party?

B: To tell you the truth, the host was very considerate. And we could use either chopsticks or knives and forks, but I used chopsticks during the party. I think chopsticks are part of the Chinese food culture. If you can't use chopsticks, you will never understand the prime of the Chinese cuisine.

H: You are right, Professor Bush. Well, what else did you do after the feast?

B: Oh, after the dinner, we sat together, chatting and watching the Spring Festival Gala on TV.

H: Yeah, the Spring Festival Gala broadcast on China Central Television Station (CCTV) is an essential entertainment for the Chinese both at home and abroad. And according to the customs, each family will stay up all through the night, talking about the past and the future.

B: The Spring Festival I spent in China was a very pleasant experience. I won't forget it in my lifetime. I like China very much. If possible, I'd like to live here for the rest of my life.

H: **Thank you for saying so.** We sincerely welcome you, Professor Bush.

Task 4

🔊 Listen and Answer

You will hear five questions. Listen carefully and give an appropriate answer to each of them.

(1) _____

(2) _____

(3) _____

(4) _____

(5) _____

Task 5

Role-play

Act out the following dialogues.

【Situation A】 A guide and his foreign friend called Jane have just taken part in "The Mid-autumn Festival". They are discussing the festival together.

The guide:

☆ Asks when the festival celebration begins.

☆ Asks what people usually eat during the festival.

☆ Asks what kind of festival it is.

☆ Asks what activities are held during the festival.

Jane:

☆ Answers that the custom can be traced back as far as to the ancient Xia and Shang dynasties and it begins on the evening of the fifteenth of the eighth lunar month.

☆ Tells the guide that people like to send and eat mooncakes as gifts in expression of their best wishes of family reunion.

☆ Says that it is a traditional festival in China.

☆ Says that people will have a family reunion feast in the evening, while looking up at the moon to extend best wishes to their relatives and friends.

【Situation B】 You are going to spend the Lantern Festival with your foreign friends, who don't know anything about this festival. So you tell them all what you know.

【Situation C】 You are discussing some traditional festivals of people of national minorities (e.g. the Water Splashing Festival) with your foreign friends. You tell your friends about the customs of these festivals.

Model 3
Peking Opera 京剧

Task 1

Warm-up

Work in pairs. Think about the following question and discuss with your partner.

What forms of entertainment can be found in Chinese theater? Give some examples and try to describe them in detail.

Task 2

Learning Points

Listen to the following *words, phrases,* and *useful expressions* and read along. Then try to memorize them.

🔊 **Words and Phrases**

appreciate	v.	欣赏，感激
differentiate	v.	区别，差别
elegant	adj.	优雅的，精美的
sleeve	n.	袖子
encyclopedia	n.	百科全书
monk	n.	僧侣，修道士
disciple	n.	弟子，门徒
overcome	v.	克服
destination	n.	目的地
be composed of		由……组成
leave a deep impression on		给……留下深刻印象
stand for		代表

Item 11 Tour of Chinese Characteristic Culture

be regarded as 被……认为是……
refer to 涉及（参考，指的是）

🔊 Useful Expressions

1. But I have no idea about it.
   但是我对它一点都不了解。
2. It's my pleasure.
   我很乐意。
3. It sounds very interesting.
   听起来很有趣。
4. Monkey Subdues the White-Bone Demon.
   孙悟空制伏白骨精。
5. It will do me good to know something about the story in advance.
   事先知晓一些故事情节对我有好处。

Task 3

🔊 Dialogue III

Listen to *Dialogue III* for the first time. Then practise the dialogue by reading it aloud with your partner. Read through it at least twice, changing your role each time.

Peking Opera

A: Hi, Jack. Nice to see you.
B: Hello, Jane. Nice to see you, too. Are you free this Sunday evening?
A: Sure.
B: Good. I want to invite you to appreciate Peking Opera at the Grand Theater.
A: Great. I was told that Peking Opera is marvelous. **But I have no idea about it.** Could you tell me something about it?
B: **It's my pleasure.** Peking Opera is quite different from other performances, in that it is composed of all kinds of performances including singing, dancing, acting, and talking, with very graceful music.
A: It's really great entertainment. Is it very popular in China?
B: Yes. It is called a national opera in China and also has become the most influential one both at home and abroad. Besides, it has left a deep impression on foreigners.
A: How about the actors and actresses?

B: The roles in Peking Opera are strictly differentiated into fixed character types: Sheng (male characters), Dan (female characters), Jing (painted faces), and Chou (male clowns). Their faces are painted in various colors, which stand for different characters.

A: **It sounds very interesting.**

B: Both actors and actresses are in attractive and elegant clothes with long sleeves which are regarded as an art.

A: I think it's a good chance for me to feast my eyes.

B: I hope so. By the way, I wonder why in Peking Opera, males used to play the female parts.

A: I don't know. Could you tell me why?

B: Sorry, I don't know either. But I'll refer to the encyclopedia and tell you later.

A: Never mind. What's the name of the opera we're going to see?

B: **"Monkey Subdues the White-Bone Demon".**

A: Could you tell me about it in detail, otherwise, I'll be totally confused.

B: This is a typical and traditional Peking Opera. The main idea of the story lies in the close relationship between a monk and his three disciples. On their way to India, they meet many unexpected difficulties and the three disciples act differently.

A: What'll happen at last?

B: Of course, they overcome all the difficulties and successfully reach the destination.

A: **It will do me good to know something about the story in advance.** Thank you for telling me so much.

B: Not at all. I hope you'll enjoy yourself on Sunday evening. See you then.

A: See you.

Task 4

🔊 Listen and Answer

You will hear five questions. Listen carefully and give an appropriate answer to each of them.

(1) _____

(2) _____

(3) _____

(4) _____

(5) _____

Task 5

Role-play

Act out the following dialogues.

【Situation A】 Zhang Hui and his foreign friend Williams have just watched a masterpiece of Peking Opera. Now they are talking about Peking Opera.

Zhang Hui:
☆ Asks whether Williams enjoyed the opera or not.
☆ Tells the history, development, and characters of Peking Opera.
☆ Feels glad to help Williams to understand Chinese culture.

Williams:
☆ Feels marvelous about the opera.
☆ Wants to know more about the Peking Opera, such as its history, development, and characters.
☆ Expresses puzzlement about something.
☆ Thanks for helping him.

【Situation B】 You and your foreign friends are talking about Chinese opera and Western opera respectively. You discuss the differences between them.

Model 4
China—Home of Tea 茶乡中国

Task 1

Learning Points

Listen to the following *words, phrases,* and *useful expressions* and read along. Then try to memorize them.

🔊 **Words and Phrases**

porcelain	*n.*	瓷器
data	*n.*	资料，数据
beverage	*n.*	饮料
entertain	*v.*	款待
process	*v.*	加工
jasmine	*n.*	茉莉
oolong	*n.*	乌龙茶
fermentation	*n.*	发酵
bake	*v.*	烘焙，烤
partial	*adj.*	部分的
border	*n.*	边缘
compress	*v.*	压缩，压榨
brew	*v.*	酿造
utensil	*n.*	器具
flavor	*n.*	风味
steep	*v.*	浸泡，浸透
minimal	*adj.*	最小的
workshop	*n.*	车间，工作室
be classified into		把……分成……
on the basis of		在……的基础上
in the course of		在……的过程中

Item 11 Tour of Chinese Characteristic Culture

comrpise of   由……组成

🔊 Useful Expressions

1. …which makes China the homeland of tea, and the country that first grew tea, made tea and discovered the effects of drinking tea.
   ……中国是第一个种植茶叶、制作茶叶和发现饮茶功效的国家，被称为茶叶之乡。
2. Chinese tea may be classified into five kinds according to the different methods by which it is processed.
   中国茶根据其不同的加工方法可以分成五类。
3. Green tea is made by firing tea leaves, keeping the original color of the tea leaves without fermentation during processing.
   绿茶是由烧制茶叶制作成的，在加工的过程中同时注意保持茶叶的原始色泽，并保留香味。
4. The most noticeable ones are the making of tea, the way of brewing, and the drinking utensils.
   最著名的就是茶叶的制作、泡茶的方法和茶具。
5. In order to let tourists have a better understanding of Chinese tea and tea culture, some scenic areas have preserved tea process workshops.
   为了让游客对中国茶及其文化有更好的认识，一些景区还保留了茶叶制作工厂。

Task 2

🔊 Passage Reading

Listen to the short passage for the first time. Then practise it by reading it aloud by yourself.

China—Home of Tea

    Chinese tea, together with silk and porcelain, began to be well-known all over the world more than a thousand years ago, and has always been an important Chinese export. According to historical data, China began to grow tea about two thousand years ago, **which makes China the homeland of tea, and the country that first grew tea, made tea, and discovered the effects of drinking tea.** People throughout China drink tea almost everyday. Tea is also the most popular beverage to entertain guests in China.

    In general, **Chinese tea may be classified into five kinds according**

to the different methods by which it is processed, i.e., green tea, black tea, jasmine tea, oolong tea, and brick tea.

Green tea is made by firing tea leaves and keeping the original color of the tea leaves without fermentation during processing.

Black tea, known as "red tea" in Chinese, needs fermentation before baking. It's developed on the basis of the green tea.

Jasmine tea is made by mixing jasmine flowers in tea leaves in the course of processing. Jasmine tea is well-known favorite of the northerners of China.

Oolong tea, a variety halfway between the green and the black teas, is made after partial fermentation. It's a specialty in Fujian Province.

Brick tea is mainly supplied to the people living in the border areas of the country. It's so called because the tea is always compressed into a form of bricks, which is good for transport and storage. Brick tea is black in color, so it is also known as "black tea" in China.

Tea-drinking is an art in China. This art comprises of many aspects. **The most noticeable ones are the making of tea, the way of brewing, and the drinking utensils.** Tea is best brewed with water that has just come to the boil. It should be made in small amounts to keep the flavor from escaping. To make tea, porcelain pots are usually the best to use. The boiling water is poured over the leaves in the pot and the teapot is quickly covered to steep for several minutes. In this way, the fragrance remains there, and the tea tastes the best.

In order to let tourists have a better understanding of Chinese tea and tea culture, some scenic areas have preserved tea process workshops. Tourists can see various procedures of tea processing and even try their hands to experience how tea is processed.

Task 3

🔊 Listen and Answer

You will hear five questions. Listen carefully and give an appropriate answer to each of them.

(1) _____

(2) _____

(3) _____

(4) _____

(5) _____

Item 11 Tour of Chinese Characteristic Culture

Task 4

Oral Practice

Retell the text in your own words.

Task 5

More Oral and Listening Practice:
【Listening】 Listen to the following dialogues and fill in the blanks.

Listening I

Traditional Chinese Festivals

A: Tomorrow is a _____ Chinese festival, the Dragon Boat Festival. _____ my hometown to eat Zongzi?

B: Great, thank you! Do you _____ the Dragon Boat Festival?

A: Yes, we have holidays on festivals such as the _____ _____, the Dragon Boat Festival and _____.

B: Are the holidays long? How many days?

A: The statutory holidays for the Spring Festival and National Day are 3 days, while those for Labor Day and the Dragon Boat Festival are 1 day. My family ____ _____ during this year's Spring Festival.

B: Spring Festival is _____ in China, isn't it?

A: Yes, it is. It's _____ in your country.

B: What other traditional festivals does China have?

A: There are Lantern Festival, Mid-autumn Festival, Qingming Festival and so on.

B: _____ do you have at the festivals?

A: We have, for example, Jiaozi, Yuanxiao, and mooncake.

Listening II

Going to a Dragon Dance

A: Hello, Mr. Brown, _____.

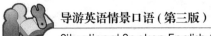

B: Yes?
A: Would you please tell your _____ that tonight we are going to enjoy a Dragon Dance at Tianyi Square?
B: A Dragon Dance?
A: Have you ever heard of it?
B: Yes, but I think it must be scary to see a monster _____.
A: Oh, you're quite _____. China's legendary dragon is not the monster encountered in Western mythology, but a benign creature symbolizing _____.
B: Really?
A: Yes. In ancient times, dragon _____ bring rain in times of drought, _____ misfortune, and bring good luck to all who need its help. This is why the dragon dance has become the most popular form of _____ at the _____ festivals, especially during _____.
B: It must have a long history then.
A: You're right. The custom can be _____ at least to the Han Dynasty some _____ years ago. Usually, five to nine dragons danced together because in China the numbers five and nine _____ _____ and nobility.
B: OK. Miss Lan, I will tell everyone in the group not to miss it. _____ _____.
A: _____. See you at 7:00 p.m. then.
B: See you.

【Topics】Divide the class into groups. Choose one of the following topics to discuss in each group. Give a short report about the group's opinion after that.

1. There are many similarities and differences between Chinese and western etiquette, can you list some examples?
2. Do you consider it necessary to protect our traditional culture, such as operas, folk music, arts, etc.?
3. Chinese people entitle foods with symbolic meanings: People enjoy noodles which symbolize longevity on their birthday party; they sit around the hot pot in a circle, which represents happiness and reunion, and they will add some sweets, Chinese dates and chestnuts in the fillings of some dumplings to express their wishes. Can you cite more foods entitled with special meanings?

Item 12

Shopping 旅游购物

- **Model 1**
  Chinese Calligraphy 中国书法

- **Model 2**
  Antiques and Ancient Furniture 古玩家具

- **Model 3**
  Shopping Service 购物服务

- **Model 4**
  Jade Culture 玉器文化

Model 1
Chinese Calligraphy 中国书法

Task 1

Warm-up

Work in pairs. Try to answer the questions below.
1. Do you know about the Four Treasures of the Study?
2. Can you list out some famous calligraphers in ancient China?

Task 2

Learning Points

Listen to the following *words, phrases,* and *useful phrases and expressions* and read along. Then try to memorize them.

🔊 **Words and Phrases**

acknowledge	v.	承认
treasure	n	财富，财宝
stick	n.	棍，棒，杖
slab	n.	厚板，平板；厚片
calligraphy	n.	书法；笔迹
innovative	adj.	创新的
drive to…		驱车前往……

🔊 **Useful Expressions**

1. As planned for today...
   根据今天的计划……

2. I have been looking forward to this the day for a long time.
   我期待这一天已经很久了。
3. What sort of things do they want to buy?
   他们想买些什么呢?
4. The most famous handicrafts are the writing brush, ink stick, paper, and ink slab.
   最著名的手工艺品是笔、墨、纸、砚。
5. Chinese calligraphy represents this historic innovative process.
   中国书法体现了这一历史创新的过程。

Task 3

Dialogue I

Listen to *Dialogue I* for the first time. Then practise the dialogue by reading it aloud with your partner. Read through it at least twice, changing your role each time.

Chinese Calligraphy

【Scene】 *Mr. Zhang, the local guide and Mrs. Smith are driving to the Ancient Culture Street.*

A: Mrs. Smith   B: Mr. Zhang

A: Good morning, Mr. Zhang.
B: Good morning, Mrs. Smith. **As planned for today,** we are going to drive to the Ancient Culture Street.
A: Oh, **I have been looking forward to this day for a long time!** Chinese five-thousand-year civilization and its rich record of characters have been acknowledged by the world. Many friends asked me to buy some Chinese ancient culture things for them.
B: **What sort of things do they want to buy?**
A: A good friend told me that she hoped to get the so-called "four treasures of the study". Frankly, I don't know about them.
B: **The most famous handicrafts are the writing brush, ink stick, paper, and ink slab.** Artists often use them to create the beautiful calligraphy.
A: I see. They are the tools of Chinese artists.
B: As we all know, in this long river of history, **Chinese calligraphy represents this historic innovative process.** Many foreign friends coming to China are surprised at the tools when artists are creating calligraphy.

A: What time shall we set out?
B: Well, our car is waiting for us just outside in the parking lot. Shall we go to the Ancient Culture Street?
A: Yes. Please.

Task 4

Listen and Answer

You will hear five questions. Listen carefully and give an appropriate answer to each of them.

(1) _____

(2) _____

(3) _____

(4) _____

(5) _____

Task 5

Role-play

Act out the following dialogues.

【Situation A】 A tour guide is now introducing the Chinese Calligraphy to Mr. Jones.

Tour guide:

☆ Greets Mr. Jones.

☆ Says that they will visit the Chinese Calligraphy shop.

☆ Introduces the local Chinese Calligraphy shop to Mr. Jones.

☆ Offers information about the Chinese Calligraphy and its characteristic with its historic background in consideration.

Mr. Jones:

☆ Greets the tour guide.

☆ Asks for the activity planned for today.

☆ Wants to know the famous local Chinese Calligraphy shop.

☆ Wants to know more information about the Chinese Calligraphy.

【 **Situation B** 】 A guide is introducing the Chinese silk handicraft (including it's history, how to make it, and what is usually drawn on it) to the foreign tourists.

Model 2
Antiques and Ancient Furniture 古玩家具

Task 1

Warm-up

Work in pairs. Match the words in column A with those in column B.

Column A	Column B
1. seal	a. 陶器
2. calligraphy and painting	b. 泥塑
3. teapoy	c. 印章
4. cupboard	d. 字画
5. clay figure	e. 茶几
6. pottery	f. 橱柜

1. (   )   2. (   )   3. (   )   4. (   )   5. (   )   6. (   )

Task 2

Learning Points

Listen to the following *words, phrases,* and *useful expressions* and read along. Then try to memorize them.

🔊 **Words and Phrases**

coin	n.	钱币
fake	adj.	仿制的，伪造的
genuine	adj.	真的
reproduction	n.	复制品

mark	v.	标志，标记
look around		四处看看，随便转转
flower-and-bird painting		花鸟画
landscape painting		山水画
be marked down		打折

🔊 Useful Expressions

1. I want to look around first with my tourists.
   我想和我的游客们先看看。
2. Shall I show you around and explain the antiques to you?
   需要我带你们看看并向你们介绍这些古董吗?
3. How about these ones?
   这些怎么样?
4. Their prices are very reasonable.
   它们的价格非常公道。
5. This can be marked down by 20%.
   这个可以打八折。
6. You are a good bargainer.
   你可真会讨价还价。
7. But you will have to pay for the postage.
   但是邮费得自付。

Task 3

🔊 Dialogue II

Listen to *Dialogue II* for the first time. Then practise the dialogue by reading it aloud with your partner. Read through it at least twice, changing your role each time.

Antiques and Ancient Furniture

A: shop assistant   B: guide

A:　Good afternoon. Can I help you?
B:　Good afternoon. **I want to look around first with my tourists.**
A:　**Shall I show you around and explain the antiques to you?**
B:　Thank you. What are these?

A: These are old coins of the Tang Dynasty.

B: Ah, I see. And what is this?

A: It is a lacquer screen with Chinese traditional paintings. Do you like it?

B: Yes. I like it, and I'd like to buy some paintings. Do you have good ones?

A: Yes. **How about these ones?** These are landscapes and these are flower-and-bird paintings.

B: They are beautiful. The horses in this picture look alive. Who painted it?

A: Xu Beihong. He was one of the most famous painters in China.

B: Is it genuine?

A: No, it is a reproduction. The real one is very expensive. All our reproductions are marked and priced. **Their prices are very reasonable.**

B: How much is it?

A: It is 500 yuan.

B: That is too much. I was born in 1954. My Chinese friend said that I was born in the year of the horse. That is why I like this painting the most.

A: All right, **this can be marked down by 20%.**

B: Can it be marked down a little bit more? I won't take it until it is marked down to 30%.

A: **You are a good bargainer.** All right, that is 350 yuan.

B: Can I have it shipped to the United States?

A: Certainly, **but you will have to pay for the postage.**

Task 4

🔊 Listen and Answer

You will hear five questions. Listen carefully and give an appropriate answer to each of them.

(1) _____

(2) _____

(3) _____

(4) _____

(5) _____

Item 12 Shopping

Task 5

Role-play

Act out the following dialogues.

【Situation A】 The tour guide is showing the tourists around the antique shop.

Shop assistant:
- ☆ Welcomes the tourists and the guide.
- ☆ Gives a brief introduction about the antiques in the shop.
- ☆ Gives a vivid introduction about the things which the tourists are interested.
- ☆ Explains whether the items are genuine or not.
- ☆ Offers the price.

Tour guide:
- ☆ Shows tourists around the shop.
- ☆ Inquires about the items in which tourists are interested in detail.
- ☆ Helps the tourists to bargain.

Tourists:
- ☆ Ask the shop assistant to give a general introduction to the items available.
- ☆ Express special interest in certain items.
- ☆ Inquire whether the items are genuine or not.
- ☆ Ask about the price.
- ☆ Bargain with the shop assistant.

【Situation B】 At the antique shop, a tourist wants to buy a piece of ancient Chinese furniture—a writing desk. You are asked to help the customer in selecting and buying the item they desire.

【Situation C】 At the antique shop, a tourist wants to buy some ancient coins. You are asked to help the customer in selecting and buying the coins they are interested in.

Model 3
Shopping Service 购物服务

Task 1

Warm-up

Work in groups. Learn the following words in the table. Then answer the questions below.

wood carving	ivory	marble	bronze
crystal	glass	paper-made	fabric

1. List some types of souvenirs that are made by those materials above.
2. Can you provide other kinds of materials that can be used in making a souvenir?

Task 2

Learning Points

Listen to the following *words, phrases,* and *useful expressions* and read along. Then try to memorize them.

🔊 Words and Phrases

commodity	*n.*	商品
specialty	*n.*	特产
jewelry	*n.*	珠宝
artwork	*n.*	工艺品
antique	*n.*	古董
pottery	*n.*	陶器
porcelain	*n.*	瓷器

musk	n.	麝香
regulation	n.	规则
ornament	n.	装饰品
purchase	v.	购买
currency	n.	货币
quantity	n.	数量
invoice	n.	账单
provision	n.	提供
authority	n.	权威
commercial street		商业街
deer antler		鹿茸
caterpillar fungus		冬虫夏草
special receipt		特种发票
the People's Bank of China		中国人民银行
Chinese patent drug		中成药
exchange memo		外汇兑换单
export sale		外销

🔊 Useful Expressions

1. On this commercial street, you can buy various commodities including local specialties, jewelry, artworks, medicinal materials, and antiques.
   这条街货品齐全，有当地特产、珠宝黄金、工艺品、药材和古董等。

2. You will see various commodities with distinctive culture, including artworks such as fans, pottery, calligraphy works, paintings, porcelain as well as coins and antiques.
   这条商业街有很多特色文化商品，工艺品类有扇子、陶器、字画、瓷器等，古董类有钱币、古玩。

3. You can also buy numerous precious medicinal materials such as deer antler, musk, and caterpillar fungus, as well as various local specialties and jewelry.
   药材类商品齐全，有鹿茸、麝香、冬虫夏草等名贵药材；还有各式各样当地特产和珠宝，任由大家选购。

4. According to Chinese law, gold and silver ornaments taken out of China by tourists shall be inspected and cleared by the customs upon the showing of a "Special Receipt" issued by the People's Bank of China.
   根据中国法律规定，旅游者携带或托运出境金银制品时，海关验凭中国人民银行所制发"特种发票"放行。

5. If the Chinese medicinal materials or Chinese patent drugs, purchased with foreign currency, for self-use and in the required quantity, are taken out by inbound tourists, they shall be inspected and cleared by the customs upon the showing of the relevant

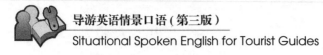

invoice and exchange memo.

入境游客出境时，携带用外汇购买数量合理、自用的中药材或中成药，海关凭相关发货票和外汇兑换水单放行。

6. Musk and other Chinese medicinal materials and Chinese patent drugs that are beyond the limits of the above-mentioned provisions shall not be allowed to exit.

麝香和超出上述规定限制金额的中药材、中成药不准携带出境。

Task 3

🔊 Dialogue III

Listen to *Dialogue III* for the first time. Then practise the dialogue by reading it aloud with your partner. Read through it at least twice, changing your role each time.

Shopping Service

【Scene】 *The tour guide Huang Lan and the tour leader Sherry are taking a group of foreign visitors to Drum Tower Commercial Street.*

G: guide   T: tourist

G: Attention please. Now we are coming to Drum Tower Commercial Street, the most bustling travel and shopping street in Ningbo. Located downtown, Drum Tower was originally the southern gate of the Zicheng City in the Tang and Song Dynasties. **On this commercial street, you can buy various commodities including local specialties, jewelry, artworks, medicinal materials, and antiques.**

T: Good! We will have a marvelous shopping experience.

G: **You will see various commodities with distinctive culture, including artworks such as fans, pottery, calligraphy works, paintings, porcelain as well as coins and antiques. You can also buy numerous precious medicinal materials such as deer antler, musk, and caterpillar fungus, as well as various local specialties and jewelry.**

T: OK. We will buy them for our family and friends.
    Ms. Huang, can you tell us the regulations on buying gold and silver ornaments?

G: While you purchase gold and silver as well as their ornaments, please keep well the "special receipt". **According to Chinese law, gold and silver ornaments taken out of China by tourists shall be inspected and cleared** by the customs upon the showing of a "Special Receipt" issued by the People's Bank of China.

T: Is there any special regulation on the purchase of Chinese medicinal materials?

G: According to the regulation on the purchase of Chinese medicinal materials: the total value of Chinese medicinal materials and Chinese patent drugs taken by tourists to foreign countries shall be limited to 300 yuan; the total value of the above materials taken to Hong Kong and Macao is 150 yuan. **If the Chinese medicinal materials or Chinese patent drugs, purchased with foreign currency, for self-use and in the required quantity, are taken out by inbound tourists, they shall be inspected and cleared by the customs upon the showing of the relevant invoice and exchange memo. Musk and other Chinese medicinal materials and Chinese patent drugs that are beyond the limits of the above-mentioned provisions shall not be allowed to exit.**

Please take care of your personal properties and safety during the shopping. We will gather here two hours later.

T: All right.

Task 4

Listen and Answer

You will hear five questions. Listen carefully and give an appropriate answer to each of them.

(1) _____
(2) _____
(3) _____
(4) _____
(5) _____

Task 5

Role-play

Act out the following dialogues.

【Situation A】 The tour guide is taking a group of foreign visitors to commercial street.

The tour guide:
☆ Tells the visitors that they are going to a commercial street.
☆ Introduces the commercial street.
☆ Introduces various commodities.
☆ Explains the regulations on buying gold and silver ornaments.
☆ Explains the regulations on the purchase of Chinese medicinal materials.
☆ Explains the regulations on the purchase of antiques.

Foreign visitor:
☆ Expresses a desire to go shopping.
☆ Asks what commodities they can buy.
☆ Asks about the regulations on buying gold and silver ornaments.
☆ Asks about the regulations on the purchase of Chinese medicinal materials.
☆ Asks about the regulations on the purchase of antiques.
☆ Expresses thanks.

【Situation B】 You are a tour guide who is escorting the tourists to a souvenir shop in your hometown. You are supposed to help them in buying souvenirs.

Model 4
Jade Culture 玉器文化

Task 1

Learning Points

Listen to the following *words, phrases,* and *useful expressions* and read along. Then try to memorize them.

🔊 **Words and Phrases**

Neolithic	*adj.*	新石器时代的
archeologist	*n.*	考古学家
excavate	*v.*	开凿，挖掘
worship	*v.*	崇拜，仰慕
preserve	*v.*	保存，防腐；保留
exceed	*v.*	超过（限度、范围）
merit	*n.*	价值；优点
dignity	*n.*	威严；高贵；体面
utensil	*n.*	器具
accessory	*n.*	零件，附件
ritual	*adj.*	仪式的
commodity	*n.*	[常]日用品
boom	*v.*	（物价）暴涨，繁荣
bestow	*v.*	给予，授，赠，赐

🔊 **Useful Expressions**

1. Chinese people first began to know and use jade in the early Neolithic period (about 5000 B.C.) according to archaeologists' findings.
   根据考古学家研究发现，中国人最早于新石器时代早期（公元前5000年左右）开始用玉。

2. Although other materials like gold, silver, and bronze were also used, none of these have ever exceeded the spiritual position that jade has acquired in people's minds.
   尽管也有使用金银铜等金属，但却没有一种金属可以取代玉在人们心目中的地位。
3. By the Shang and Zhou dynasties, jade wares had been developed into tools, weapons, daily utensils, accessories, and ritual utensils.
   到了商周时期，玉已经被用来制造工具、武器、日用品、配饰和祭祀用品。
4. For thousands of years untill now, jade has been and is a symbol of love and virtue as well as status.
   数千年来，玉一直是爱、美德与地位的象征。

Task 2

🔊 Passage Reading II

Listen to the short passage for the first time. Then practise it by reading it aloud by yourself.

Jade Culture

The history of jade is as old as the Chinese civilization. **Chinese people first began to know and use jade in the early Neolithic period (about 5000 B.C.) according to archaeologists' findings**, represented by the Hemudu culture in Zhejiang Province, and from the middle and late Neolithic period, represented by the Hongshan culture along the Liao River, the Longshan culture along the Yellow River, and the Yangshao culture in the Tai Lake region.

Many jade wares dating back to 4,000 to 6,000 years ago have been excavated in different places. It changed from the use of decoration into other uses, such as the rites of worship and burial. Jade is believed to have the function of preserving the body after death and has been found in emperors' tombs from thousands of years ago. One tomb contained an entire suit made of jade, to ensure the physical immortality of its owner. **Although other materials like gold, silver, and bronze were also used, none of these have ever exceeded the spiritual position that jade has acquired in people's minds**——it is associated with merit, morality, grace, and dignity.

By the Shang and Zhou dynasties, jade wares had been developed into tools, weapons, daily utensils, accessories, and ritual utensils. As commodity exchange boomed, jade was bestowed with a currency function. **For thousands of years untill now, jade has been and is a symbol of love and virtue as well as status.**

Task 3

◄)) Listen and Answer

You will hear five questions. Listen carefully and give an appropriate answer to each of them.

(1) _____

(2) _____

(3) _____

(4) _____

(5) _____

Task 4

Oral Practice

Retell the text in your own words.

Task 5

More Oral and Listening Practice:

【Listening】 Listen to the dialogues and fill in the blanks.

◄)) Listening I

At the Jewelry's Store

A: Can I help you, madam?

B: Yes, I'd like _____ for my friends.

A: Would you like jewelry? Today is _____ and all the jewelry is on sale at Rich's store.

B: That's great. _____ jewels?

A: Yes, we have 24K and _____ gold necklaces, chains, and earrings.

B: May I have a look?

A: Sure. _____. Its regular price is _____, and

now you can have it with a twenty percent discount.

B: It's very elegant. _____.
A: All right. Is there anything else you want?
B: Will you show me that _____?
A: Yes, here you are.

Listening II

At the Shop

A: Good morning, sir. May I help you?
B: Yes, can you _____?
A: How about some dolls? Girls at that age are especially _____.
B: She has already got plenty of dolls. I'd like to _____ this time.
A: Maybe you can buy her a watch. You see, I have a _____ of watches.
B: This is a good idea. Can you _____ for me?
A: This kind of watch is _____. It's very popular among children. Furthermore, the _____ and it is cheap, too.
B: I suppose my daughter will like it. _____?
A: 25 dollars.
B: Well, could you wrap it up for me?
A: Certainly. I'm sure your daughter _____ watch.
B: Thank you.
A: You're welcome.

【Topics】Divide the class into groups. Choose one of the following topics to discuss in each group. Give a short report about the group's opinion after that.

1. Why can't the poor people benefit from the development of tourism?
2. In which aspects do you think we should improve to set up a perfect tourism market?
3. Do you think it worthwhile to protect cultural relics? Why?

Item 13

Handling Problems & Emergencies
处理问题与紧急情况

- Model 1
  A Delayed Flight 航班延误

- Model 2
  Calling the First Aid Center 打电话到急救中心

- Model 3
  First Aid Techniques 急救技术

Model 1
A Delayed Flight 航班延误

Task 1

Warm-up

Work in pairs. If you are a guide, how will you handle the problems of delayed transportation? Discuss with your partner.

Task 2

Learning Points

Listen to the following *words, phrases,* and *useful expressions* and read along. Then try to memorize them.

🔊 Words and Phrases

foggy	*adj.*	有雾的，多雾的
amazing	*adj.*	令人惊异的
reception	*n.*	接待
due to		归因于
clear away		消散
kill the time		打发时间

🔊 Useful Expressions

1. The staff here told me that the flight had been delayed due to the foggy weather.
   机场工作人员告诉我因为大雾天气，航班延误了。
2. The weather report said that the fog will be cleared away in 2 hours.
   天气预报说大雾在 2 个小时内就会消散。

3. I'm afraid so.
   恐怕是的。
4. Why don't we kill the time by looking around the shops and stores here?
   我们可以在这里的商铺逛逛打发时间。
5. Maybe you will find something amazing!
   也许你能发现一些很不错的东西!
6. And it offers a large variety of antiques including: coins, pottery, and traditional Chinese paintings.
   那里面有各种古董,包括钱币、瓷器和传统中国画。

Task 3

Dialogue I

Listen to *Dialogue I* for the first time. Then practise the dialogue by reading it aloud with your partner. Read through it at least twice, changing your role each time.

A Delayed Flight

【Scene】 *In the airport lobby, Zhang Hua, a young tour guide from the China Travel Service, is explaining to John Smith about the delayed flight that he will take.*

J: John Smith   Z: Zhang Hua

J: Excuse me, did flight number FU88099 arrive? I have been waiting here for an hour. And it should have arrived half an hour ago. What happened?
Z: I don't know, but I will ask the reception desk for it.
   (several minutes later)
Z: **The staff here told me that the flight had been delayed due to the foggy weather.**
J: Oh, it's terrible. Did they say when exactly will the flight arrive?
Z: **The weather report said that the fog will be cleared away in 2 hours.**
J: That's to say we have to wait for another 90 minutes?
Z: **I'm afraid so.**
J: It's quite a long time to be here waiting for the flight.
Z: **Why don't we kill the time by looking around the shops and stores here? Maybe you will find something amazing!**
J: That's a good idea! Is there any antique shop around here?
Z: Yes, it is just around the corner over there. **And it offers a large variety of antiques including: coins, pottery, and traditional Chinese paintings.** What do you want to buy?

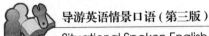

J: I just want to have a look around there.
Z: OK, let's go!

Task 4

🔊 Listen and Answer

You will hear five questions. Listen carefully and give an appropriate answer to each of them.

(1) _____

(2) _____

(3) _____

(4) _____

(5) _____

Task 5

Role-play

Act out the following dialogues.

【Situation A】 Mr. Black, a tourist, is now complaining about the delayed flight to the tour guide at the airport.

Mr. Black:

☆ Complains to the tour guide.

☆ Asks about the arrival time.

☆ Shows anxiety.

☆ Asks if there are some other things to do.

☆ Suggests going to visit the nearest souvenir shop.

Tour guide:

☆ Promises to ask for the reason.

☆ Gives the reason why it's delayed.

☆ Gives the possible time when the flight will come.

☆ Suggests looking around to kill the time.

☆ Shows the nearest souvenir shop to Mr. Black.

【Situation B】 At the bus station, a foreign business traveler is complaining about the delayed bus to the tour guide.

Item 13 Handling Problems & Emergencies

Model 2
Calling the First Aid Center 打电话到急救中心

Task 1

Warm-up

Work in pairs. Learn the following words and answer the question below.

ache	bleed	faint	influenza	diarrhea
dispensary	blood bank	outpatient department		
inpatient department		registration office		

What will you do if the tourists get ill on the trip?

Task 2

Learning Points

Listen to the following *words*, *phrases*, and *useful expressions* and read along. Then try to memorize them.

🔊 **Words and Phrases**

ambulance	n.	救护车
urgent	adj.	紧急的
acute	adj.	急性的
appendicitis	n.	阑尾炎
stretcher	n.	担架
bathe	n.	清洗，洗澡
remove	v.	移除
right away		立即，马上

suffer from 承受痛苦
emergency ward 急救室

🔊 Useful Expressions

1. Please send an ambulance to 68 Hunan Road.
   请派一辆救护车到湖南路68号。
2. I think the patient is suffering from acute appendicitis.
   我认为病人可能得了急性阑尾炎。
3. He's very ill.
   他病得很厉害。
4. What's the trouble with him, doctor?
   他到底怎么了?
5. When can I take care of him?
   我什么时候可以照顾他?

Task 3

🔊 Dialogue II

Listen to *Dialogue II* for the first time. Then practise the dialogue by reading it aloud with your partner. Read through it at least twice, changing your role each time.

Calling the First Aid Center

【Scene】 *A foreign visitor is suffering from acute appendicitis. Now the tour guide is calling the first aid center for help.*

T: tour guide   H: hospital receiver   D: doctor

T: Is this the Friendship Hospital? **Please send an ambulance to 68 Hunan Road.**
H: Is it urgent? Our ambulances are not enough to meet every call.
T: Of course. It's urgent. **I think the patient is suffering from acute appendicitis.** He may die if not treated in time.
H: All right, we'll come right away.
   (After a while…)
H: Where's the patient?
T: He's in the room. **He's very ill.**

Item 13 Handling Problems & Emergencies

H: Don't worry. We'll put him in the stretcher. Are you coming with us? Step in please.
D: Carry him into the emergency ward. Here we are.
T: I'm his guide. **What's the trouble with him, doctor?**
D: He has appendicitis, but is all right now since it was removed. He'll have to rest for a few weeks to recover.
T: May I send food for him?
D: No, outside food is not permitted.
T: **When can I take care of him?**
D: Our nurse can take good care of him.

Task 4

🔊 Listen and Answer

You will hear five questions. Listen carefully and give an appropriate answer to each of them.

(1) _____

(2) _____

(3) _____

(4) _____

(5) _____

Task 5

Role-play

Act out the following dialogues.

【Situation A】 You are an English tour guide who is calling the first aid center for a medical care of a sick tourist.

Tour guide:
☆ Calls the first aid center.
☆ Asks them to send an ambulance.
☆ Tells them that the patient is very ill.
☆ Asks when they can take care of the patient again.

Hospital receiver:
☆ Answers the phone.
☆ Explains that the ambulance is in limited numbers.
☆ Tells the guide that they will send one.
☆ Asks for the accurate address.

Doctor:
☆ Performs preparation work.
☆ Asks the guide to go with him/her.
☆ Confirms the patient's situation.
☆ Responds to the guide's request.

【Situation B】 One of your tourists has gotten diarrhea, you should call the first aid center for help.

【Situation C】 One of your tourists has gotten a bad wound and is bleeding heavily, you should call the first aid center for help.

Item 13 Handling Problems & Emergencies

Model 3
First Aid Techniques 急救技术

Task 1

Learning Points

Listen to the following *words, phrases,* and *useful expressions* and read along. Then try to memorize them.

🔊 **Words and Phrases**

climate	n.	气候
zone	n.	区域，范围
artificial	adj.	人工的
respiration	n.	呼吸
straightly	adv.	笔直地
thumb	n.	拇指
forefinger	n.	食指
nip	v.	夹，捏
inhale	v.	吸气

🔊 **Useful Expressions**

1. Changes in climate and time zone as well as long hours of sightseeing may easily cause this kind of sudden heart attack.
   气候的变化、时区的更迭和长时间的观光很容易引发各类心脏疾病。
2. The most common use of FATs (First Aid Techniques) is artificial respiration.
   最常见的急救技术是人工呼吸。
3. Use the thumb and forefinger to nip the wing of the nose.
   用拇指与食指夹住鼻子。
4. After a deep inhale of air, the operator should cover the patient's mouth with his own lips and put the air into the patient's mouth slowly.
   深吸一口气，然后急救人员用嘴将空气缓缓输入病人的口腔里。

5. Do it for several times and ensure no more than 1 to 1.5 seconds between each time.
   重复数次，每次间隔不超过1～1.5秒。

Task 2

🔊 Passage Reading

Listen to the short passage for the first time. Then practise it by reading it aloud by yourself.

First Aid Techniques

Changes in climate and time zone as well as long hours of sightseeing may easily cause this kind of sudden heart attack. In order to save the tourist's life at the first moment, you should know how to give first aid to him/her. **The most common use of FATs (First Aid Techniques) is artificial respiration.** It can be performed easily in any condition.

As for artificial respiration, you should first let the patient lay on a flat ground straight. And also you should put his arms close to his body. Then, clean his mouth. After all these preparation works are finished, you can start. **Use the thumb and forefinger to nip the wing of the nose. After a deep inhale of air, the operator should cover the patient's mouth with his own lips and put the air into the patient's mouth slowly.** And make sure that the air goes into the patient's body. **Do it for several times and ensure no more than 1 to 1.5 seconds between each time.**

Task 3

🔊 Listen and Answer

You will hear five questions. Listen carefully and give an appropriate answer to each of them.

(1) _____

(2) _____

(3) _____

(4) _____

(5) _____

Item 13 Handling Problems & Emergencies

Task 4

Oral Practice

Retell the text in your own words.

Task 5

More Oral and Listening Practice:
【Listening】 Listen to the dialogues and fill in the blanks.

Listening I

The Delayed Flight

A: Hello, I have ticket for the 8:00 flight to Guangzhou.
B: I'm so sorry that the flight has been delayed due to _____.
A: When will the plane be ready for take-off?
B: Well, it could be as soon as within _____, or as late as tomorrow morning. We're so sorry to _____. And we'd like to offer you a room _____ at the hotel.
A: Where's the hotel? Is it far from here?
B: No. It's just _____.
A: Will you contact us as soon as the plane is ready?
B: Of course. We'll send a _____ to pick you up.
A: Thank you very much.

Listening II

About the Toilet

A: Maintenance Department. Can I help you?
B: Yes, there seems to be _____ with the toilet.
A: We'll send someone to repair it immediately. _____ _____?
B: _____.
A: May I come in?

B: Come in.
A: The _____ doesn't flush.
B: Let me see. Oh, it's clogged... It's _____ now. You may try it.
A: Yes, it's working now. Thank you.
B: You're welcome. _____ ?
A: _____. I can hardly sleep.
B: I'm very sorry, sir. Some part needs to be _____. I will be back soon.

【Topics】Divide the class into groups. Choose one of the following topics to discuss in each group. Give a short report about the group's opinion after that.

1. What's a guide's responsibility in coping with emergencies a tourist encounters?
2. What should the guide do to prevent the guests from being troubled by emergencies?
3. The Chinese wine culture is closely related to all kinds of social activities. List some examples to demonstrate the relationship.

Item 14

Handling Customer Complaints
顾客投诉处理服务

- **Model 1**
  Complaining about the Food   食品投诉

- **Model 2**
  A Tour Guide or a Shopping Guide   导游还是导购

- **Model 3**
  A Complaint Letter on Holiday Booking   旅游预订投诉信

Model 1
Complaining about the Food 食品投诉

Task 1

Warm-up

Work in pairs. Try to answer the question below.
What kind of food do you like (or don't like)? Why?

Task 2

Learning Points

Listen to the following *words, phrases,* and *useful expressions* and read along. Then try to memorize them.

🔊 **Words and Phrases**

lamb	*n.*	羔羊
inedible	*adj.*	不能吃的
fatty	*adj.*	油腻的
oily	*adj.*	油腻的
recommendation	*n.*	推荐
order	*v.*	点菜
discount	*n.*	折扣
roast duck		烤鸭

🔊 **Useful Expressions**

1. What's up?
   发生了什么?

2. I will call the waiter to deal with it.
   我会叫服务员来处理的。
3. I've told them to make a change for you.
   我已经让他们给您重做了一份。
4. They promised to serve you in less than 5 minutes.
   他们承诺在 5 分钟内上菜。
5. They will give us a 15% discount.
   他们会给我们打八五折。

Task 3

Dialogue I

Listen to *Dialogue I* for the first time. Then practise the dialogue by reading it aloud with your partner. Read through it at least twice, changing your role each time.

Complaining about the Food

【Scene】*A foreign tourist is complaining to the guide in a restaurant about the food.*

A: the foreign tourist   B: the guide

A: Look, the food in this restaurant is so terrible!
B: **What's up?**
A: I hate to say, but this leg of lamb is inedible. It is so fatty. And the roast duck is too oily. In fact, it's the worst I've ever eaten!
B: Mm. It did like what you say. **I will call the waiter to deal with it.**
   (Several minutes later...)
B: OK, **I've told them to make a change for you.**
A: Will I wait for a long time?
B: No. **They promised to serve you in less than 5 minutes.**
A: I also want to order a soup, What's your recommendation?
B: I heard that the egg and vegetable soup here is quite delicious.
A: Really? That's good. Could you please order one for me?
B: No problem!
   (After meal...)
A: Can we make a discount for this?
B: Of course, **they will give us a 15% discount.**
A: You are so nice!

B: You are welcome.

Task 4

Listen and Answer

You will hear five questions. Listen carefully and give an appropriate answer to each of them.

(1) _____
(2) _____
(3) _____
(4) _____
(5) _____

Task 5

Role-play

Act out the following dialogues.

【Situation A】 You are escorting Mr. Black to have dinner in a restaurant. Mr. Black isn't satisfied with the food. You are asked to help Mr. Black to solve the problem.

Mr. Black:
☆ Complains about the food.
☆ Gives vivid descriptions.
☆ Asks for the serving time.
☆ Asks for a discount.
☆ Gives thanks to the guide.

You:
☆ Asks what happened.
☆ Promises that you will help Mr. Black to solve it.
☆ Says that the problem has been solved.
☆ Tells the serving time.
☆ Tells the percentage of discount.

【Situation B】 At the restaurant, a foreign business traveler is complaining about the bad service and asking for your help.

Item 14 Handling Customer Complaints

Model 2
A Tour Guide or a Shopping Guide 导游还是导购

Task 1

Warm-up

Work in pairs. If you are a guide, when you are guiding your guests at a shop, what will you say to them? Discuss with your partner.

Task 2

Learning Points

Listen to the following *words, phrases,* and *useful expressions* and read along. Then try to memorize them.

🔊 **Words and Phrases**

unbelievable	*adj.*	难以置信的
kickback	*n.*	佣金，回扣
scenic	*adj.*	景色优美的
spot	*n.*	地点，现场
terrible	*adj.*	糟糕的
responsibility	*n.*	责任
play an important role		扮演重要角色
hold belief		持有信念

🔊 **Useful Expressions**

1. There are some indeed, but not all.
   确实有一些，但不是全部。

2. The other important reason may be that by showing tourists around the stores a lot, the guide can kill a lot of time and save a large amount of energy instead of guiding them in a scenic spot.

   另一个重要的原因可能是，导游通过多带领游客逛商店而不是带他们去旅游景点，可以消磨很多时间并节省大量的精力。

3. It wastes a lot of time and money for the tourists.

   这浪费了游客很多的时间和金钱。

4. But not all the guides act like this.

   但不是所有的导游都这样。

5. I always believe that it is our tour guide's responsibility to show beautiful scenery as well as warm and kind service to our guests.

   我一直认为导游的职责是向游客展示美丽的风景和提供热情友好的服务。

Task 3

Dialogue II

Listen to *Dialogue II* for the first time. Then practise the dialogue by reading it aloud with your partner. Read through it at least twice, changing your role each time.

A Tour Guide or a Shopping Guide

【Scene】 *A tourist is discussing with a tour escort about whether today's guide is a tour guide or a shopping guide.*

A: the tourist   B: the tour escort

A: It's unbelievable that today's tour guide prefers to guide their tourists to stores rather than to scenic spots.

B: **There are some indeed, but not all.**

A: What do you think may lead to this situation?

B: The kickback of course.

A: Yeah. Money always plays an important role in it. But do you think there is any other reason?

B: In my opinion, **the other important reason may be that by showing tourists around the stores a lot, the guide can kill a lot of time and save a large amount of energy instead of guiding them in a scenic spot.**

A: I couldn't agree with you more! But don't you think that really hurts the

Item 14 Handling Customer Complaints

tourists?

B: Yes, **it wastes a lot of time and money for the tourists.**

A: How terrible!

B: **But not all the guides act like this.** Actually, most of us do a good job on a trip. **I always believe that it is our tour guide's responsibility to show beautiful scenery as well as warm and kind service to our guests.**

A: You are right. And I hope every guide can hold the same belief like you!

B: Thank you.

Task 4

🔊 Listen and Answer

You will hear five questions. Listen carefully and give an appropriate answer to each of them.

(1) _____

(2) _____

(3) _____

(4) _____

(5) _____

Task 5

Role-play

Act out the following dialogues.

【Situation A】 You are an English tour guide who is explaining to a tourist about the responsibility of a tour guide.

Tourist:

☆ Gives impression of today's tour guide.

☆ Shows confusion about their responsibility.

☆ Asks for the reason.

☆ Shows his attitude (agree or disagree).

☆ Gives his own wish.

Guide:

☆ Makes a comment on the tourist's idea.

☆ Gives explanations.

☆ Shows your own attitude.

☆ Express thanks.

【**Situation B**】 At a store, you are answering a tourist's question about the shopping guide.

Item 14 Handling Customer Complaints

Model 3
A Complaint Letter on Holiday Booking
旅游预订投诉信

Task 1

Learning Points

Listen to the following *words, phrases,* and *useful expressions* and read along. Then try to memorize them.

🔊 Words and Phrases

arrangement	*n.*	安排
balcony	*n.*	阳台
faculty	*n.*	职员
extra	*adj.*	额外的
exhaust	*v.*	筋疲力尽，使……劳累
prompt	*adj.*	迅速的，及时的
settle	*v.*	解决
properly	*adv.*	适当地
favorable	*adj.*	满意的
favorable reply		满意的答复

🔊 Useful Expressions

1. I am writing to make a complaint about your poor arrangement of my booking which puts me in a very difficult position.
   我写投诉信是因为你们对于我的预订的糟糕处理，给我带来了很大的麻烦。
2. But when I arrived at the hotel five days ago, your staff told me there was no vacancy anymore.
   但当我5天前抵达酒店时，你们的员工告诉我没有空房间了。
3. Because your staff causes the problems, I expect you to work with me to get a

satisfactory resolution.

因为是你的员工造成了这个问题，所以我希望你能够给我一个满意的解决办法。

4. I sincerely hope that you will give prompt attention to my case and settle it properly as soon as possible.

我诚挚地希望这封信能引起您足够的重视，并能尽快解决我的问题。

Task 2

🔊 Passage Reading II

Listen to the short passage for the first time. Then practise it by reading them aloud by yourself.

A Complaint Letter on Holiday Booking

Dear sir or madam,

  I am writing to make a complaint about your poor arrangement of my booking which puts me in a very difficult position.

  I booked a single room with a balcony facing to the beach about 15 days ago. And the receiver promised me one. **But when I arrived at hotel five days ago, your staff told me there was no vacancy anymore.** It's unbelievable! And then I had to spend extra money to find another hotel to live in for the next two days, which made me feel exhausted and angry. **Because your staff causes the problems, I expect you to work with me to get a satisfactory resolution:** to give back the money to me for the two nights I spent at the other hotel.

  I sincerely hope that you will give prompt attention to my case and settle it properly as soon as possible. I am looking forward to your favorable reply.

Sincerely,
Peterson

Task 3

🔊 Listen and Answer

You will hear five questions. Listen carefully and give an appropriate answer to each of them.

Item 14 Handling Customer Complaints

(1) _____

(2) _____

(3) _____

(4) _____

(5) _____

Task 4

Oral Practice

Retell the text in your own words.

Task 5

More Oral and Listening Practice:

【Listening】 Listen to the dialogues and fill in the blanks.

Listening I

Complaining about the Facilities in the Hotel Room

A: _____!

B: What happened?

A: The facilities in my room are so poor! The air conditioning broke down when I just turned it on.

B: In that case, _____.

A: Look, that's the _____ problem! I have asked the maintenance department _____ times, but no one responded.

B: _____! They should be at their place for _____. What happened?

A: At last, I called the _____. And they told me that all their repairmen are busy now.

B: What?! All of them?

A: Yes, _____.

B: What's wrong with them? _____.

A: OK, thank you.

B: You are welcome.

Listening II

Complaining about Room Cleaning

A: Good afternoon. May I help you?

B: Good afternoon. Why has my room not been _____?

A: I am sorry. We'll _____ as soon as possible.

B: And it's so _____ that when you asked for an extra bag for dry cleaning and I was told they are unavailable.

A: Thank you for _____ this problem. I will investigate it right away.

B: Besides, when I asked for a little more variety of fruits, I was told most of the fruits were _____.

A: I'll report to the manager why you have not experienced our usual _____ _____.

B: Furthermore, the room attendant always shuts the door hard when she finishes the _____.

A: I do apologize that _____. I assure you the problems won't happen again. We are sorry again.

【Topics】Divide the class into groups. Choose one of the following topics to discuss in each group. Give a short report about the group's opinion after that.

1. What is the tour guide's role in dealing with the tourist's complaint?

2. What should you do to avoid too many complaints?

3. In order to build Beijing into a modern international city, many courtyards and hutongs in Beijing have been destroyed. Comment on this.

Item 15

Checking Out 结账退房服务

- **Model 1**
  Checking Out 退房服务

- **Model 2**
  Paying by Credit Card 信用卡付账

- **Model 3**
  Paying with a Traveler's Check 旅行支票付账

- **Model 4**
  Checkout Service Procedures 退房结账程序

Model 1
Checking Out 退房服务

Task 1

Warm-up

Work in pairs. Learn the following words about checking out at the hotel and answer the question below.

| return the room key | clear the bills | settle the bills |

What should you do if you want to check out?

Task 2

Learning Points

Listen to the following *words, phrases,* and *useful expressions* and read along. Then try to memorize them.

🔊 **Words and Phrases**

print	v.	打印
price	n.	价格
amount	n.	金额
lamp	n.	灯具
inform	v.	通知
imprint	n.	印记
sign	v.	签名
receipt	n.	收据
gather	v.	聚集

Item 15 Checking Out

bellman   *n.*   行李员
check out   退房

🔊 Useful Expressions

1. I want to check out for my group now.
   我要为我们旅游团退房。
2. What's your room number?
   你们的房号是多少？
3. Ms. Jin, you were here two days ago on the afternoon of September 18, is that right?
   金女士，你们入住的时间是两天前的 9 月 18 日下午，对吗？
4. What's this amount for?
   这个金额是什么？
5. Do you accept credit cards?
   你们接受信用卡支付吗？
6. Please sign your name on the printout.
   请您在打印单上签字。
7. Please take your credit card and keep the receipt.
   请拿好您的信用卡并且保存好收据。
8. Could you gather the luggage for my group?
   您可以帮我们团队把行李集中一下吗？

Task 3

🔊 Dialogue I

Listen to *Dialogue I* for the first time. Then practise the dialogue by reading it aloud with your partner. Read through it at least twice, changing your role each time.

Checking Out

【Scene】 *The tour guide Jin Ying is helping a group of foreign visitors to check out at a hotel in Ningbo. The reception clerk receives the tour guide.*

C: clerk   G: guide

C: Good morning, madam. May I help you?
G: Good morning. **I want to check out for my group now.** These are all the room cards.

C: May I know your name?
G: Jin Ying, the tour guide from Ningbo Youth Travel Agency.
C: **What's your room number?**
G: We stayed in Room 2101 to Room 2112.
C: OK. That's twelve rooms altogether. Yes, **Ms. Jin, you were here two days ago on the afternoon of September 18, is that right?**
G: Yes, exactly.
C: So you'll check out before 12:00?
G: Yes.
C: Just a moment, please. I will print the bill for you. Here you are. This is your bill. The total price is RMB 1,180. Please check it.
G: OK. **What's this amount for?**
C: That's for the broken lamp for Room 2108. We charge it individually. Could you inform the guest in Room 2108 to pay for it?
G: OK. **Do you accept credit cards?**
C: Yes, we do accept some major credit cards. What kind of card do you have?
G: Visa Card.
C: Fine. Let me take an imprint of it.
G: Here it is.
C: Thanks. Just wait a moment. **Please sign your name on the printout,** Ms. Jin.
G: OK. Here you are.
C: Thank you. **Please take your credit card and keep the receipt.** I hope next time you're in Ningbo you'll stay with us again.
G: I will. **Could you gather the luggage for my group?**
C: Of course. I will send the bellman to do that.
G: Thank you very much.
C: You are welcome. See you.
G: See you.

Task 4

🔊 Listen and Answer

You will hear five questions. Listen carefully and give an appropriate answer to each of them.

(1) _____

(2) _____
(3) _____
(4) _____
(5) _____

Task 5

Role-play

Act out the following dialogues.

【Situation A】 The guest is at the Front Desk and the receptionist receives him. The guest wants to check out.

The receptionist:
☆ Greets the guest.
☆ Asks the guest's name and room number.
☆ Asks if the guest has used any other service.
☆ Lets the guest wait.
☆ Prepares the guest's bill and tells the guest the total amount.
☆ Tells the guest that they have paid a deposit.
☆ Gives the guest his change and invoice.
☆ Hopes that the guests will have a good journey.

The guest:
☆ Greets the receptionist.
☆ Wants to settle the bill.
☆ Tells his name and room number.
☆ Says that he has not used any other service.
☆ Checks the bill.
☆ Gives the receptionist the receipt of the deposit.
☆ Checks the change.
☆ Says goodbye to the receptionist.

【Situation B】 Mr. Clarke checks out at the Cashier's. The clerk asks the guest to exchange his US dollars into RMB.

Model 2
Paying by Credit Card 信用卡付账

Task 1

Warm-up

Work in pairs. Learn the following words about settling the bill at the hotel. Then answer the questions below.

| credit card | cash | traveler's check |

1. How many ways could you settle the bills?
2. Have you had such experience of using credit cards to buy something before? What does the receptionist/cashier do with your credit card?

Task 2

Learning Points

Listen to the following *words, phrases,* and *useful expressions* and read along. Then try to memorize them.

🔊 Words and Phrases

cash	*n.*	现金
service	*n.*	服务
account	*n.*	账户；账号
imprint	*n.*	压印；印记
sign	*v.*	签
the Front Desk		前台

Item 15 Checking Out

🔊 Useful Expressions

1. I'd like to check out, please.
   我想要结账。
2. Your bill totals…
   您的账单总计……
3. Can I pay by my credit card?
   我能用信用卡付账吗?
4. Let me take an imprint of it.
   让我帮您压个印。
5. Please sign your name on the printout.
   请把您的名字签在打印单上。

Task 3

🔊 Dialogue II

Listen to *Dialogue II* for the first time. Then practise the dialogue by reading it aloud with your partner. Read through it at least twice, changing your role each time.

Paying with Credit Card

【Scene】 *A guest comes to the Front Desk to check out by credit card.*

S: Staff   G: Guest

S: Good morning, sir. Can I help you?
G: **I'd like to check out, please.**
S: May I know your name and room number, sir?
G: I'm Mr. John Rich, Room 1508.
S: Yes. Have you used any other hotel services this morning?
G: No, I haven't used any services and I paid cash for my breakfast.
S: Fine. One moment while I check the account. Three nights at RMB 500 each, and **your bill totals** RMB 1,500. Here you are. Have a check, please.
G: Correct. But I don't have enough cash for it. **Can I pay by my credit card?**
S: Certainly, we do accept some major credit cards. What card do you have?
G: Visa Card.
S: Fine. **Let me take an imprint of it.**
G: Here it is.

S: Thanks. Just wait a moment. **Please sign your name on the printout**, Mr. Rich.

G: OK. Here you are.

S: Thank you. Please take your credit card and keep the receipt.

Task 4

🔊 Listen and Answer

You will hear five questions. Listen carefully and give an appropriate answer to each of them.

(1) _____

(2) _____

(3) _____

(4) _____

(5) _____

Task 5

Role-play

Act out the following dialogues.

【Situation A】 The guest is at the Front Desk and the receptionist receives him. The guest wants to check out.

The receptionist:
☆ Greets the guest.
☆ Asks the guest's name and room number.
☆ Asks if the guest has used any facilities.
☆ Prepares the guest's bill.
☆ Tells the guest the total amount.
☆ Asks how the guest likes to settle the bill.
☆ Takes an imprint of the card.
☆ Asks the guest to sign the printout.
☆ Returns the credit card.
☆ Tells the guest to keep the receipt.

Item 15 Checking Out

The guest:
- ☆ Greets the receptionist.
- ☆ Wants to settle the bill.
- ☆ Tells his name and room number.
- ☆ Answers that he has paid other services in cash.
- ☆ Checks the bill.
- ☆ Tells that he would like to use the credit card.
- ☆ Gives the receptionist the card.
- ☆ Says goodbye to the receptionist.

【Situation B】At the Front Desk, the guest wants to check out by credit card and the clerk receives him.

Model 3
Paying with a Traveler's Check 旅行支票付账

Task 1

Warm-up

Work in pairs. Think about the following question and discuss with your partner.

What are the differences between paying by credit card, in cash and with a traveler's check?

Task 2

Learning Points

Listen to the following *words, phrases,* and *useful expressions* and read along. Then try to memorize them.

🔊 Words and Phrases

charge	v.	要价，支付费用
rate	n.	费用，价格
laundry	n.	洗衣物
passport	n.	护照
traveler's check		旅行支票
exchange rate		外汇牌价
exchange memo		（外汇兑换）水单

🔊 Useful Expressions

1. Were you in Room 2816?
   您住在 2816 房间？
2. One moment, please, and I'll get the bill ready.

请稍等，我把您的账单准备好。
3. Please check it.
   请您核对。
4. How would you like to pay your bill?
   您怎样支付您的账单？
5. May I see your passport, please?
   我能看下您的护照吗？
6. We hope you'll come again. Have a nice trip.
   欢迎您再来。旅途愉快！

Task 3

◆) Dialogue III

Listen to *Dialogue III* for the first time. Then practise the dialogue by reading it aloud with your partner. Read through it at least twice, changing your role each time.

Paying with a Traveler's Check

【Scene】 *A guest pays his bill with his traveler's check.*

S: staff   G: guest

S: Good morning. Can I help you, sir?
G: I'd like to check out. The name is Alan Dick.
S: Excuse me, **were you in Room 2816?**
G: That's right. May I see the bill?
S: **One moment, please, and I'll get the bill ready**… It totals RMB 5,020. Here you are. **Please check it.**
G: OK. Does this include service and tax?
S: Yes, that's everything. We charge you for the rate of the room, room service, laundry, and drinks. Is that all right, Mr. Dick?
G: Yes, I don't see any problem with it.
S: **How would you like to pay your bill?**
G: With my traveler's check, if that's OK.
S: That'll do nicely. Thank you.
G: Can you tell me the exchange rate of US dollars for traveler's checks?
S: It's RMB 720 against 100 US dollars. **May I see your passport, please?**
G: Here you are.

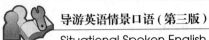

S: Please sign your name on the traveler's check and sign again on the memo.
G: OK.
S: Here is your invoice. And this is the exchange memo.
G: Thank you. Goodbye.
S: **We hope you'll come again,** Mr. Dick. **Have a nice trip.** Goodbye.

Task 4

Listen and Answer

You will hear five questions. Listen carefully and give an appropriate answer to each of them.

(1) _____

(2) _____

(3) _____

(4) _____

(5) _____

Task 5

Role-play

Act out the following dialogues.

【Situation A】 The guest is at the Front Desk and the receptionist receives him. The guest wants to check out.

The receptionist:
☆ Greets the guest.
☆ Asks the guest's name and room number.
☆ Asks if the guest has used any facilities.
☆ Prepares the guest's bill, tells the guest the total amount and explains the bill.
☆ Asks how the guest likes to settle the bill.
☆ Tells the guest the exchange rate.
☆ Asks to see the guest's passport.
☆ Gives the guest the invoice and the exchange memo.
☆ Hopes that he will come again.

Item 15 Checking Out

The guest:
- ☆ Greets the receptionist.
- ☆ Wants to settle the bill.
- ☆ Tells his name and room number.
- ☆ Answers that he has paid other services in cash.
- ☆ Checks the bill.
- ☆ Tells that he would like to use the traveler's check.
- ☆ Asks the exchange rate.
- ☆ Gives the receptionist the passport.
- ☆ Signs the name on the traveler's check and the exchange memo.
- ☆ Says goodbye to the receptionist.

【Situation B】 Mr. Brown checks out at the reception. When the room attendant checks the rooms, she finds two bath towels missing.

Model 4
Checkout Service Procedures 退房结账程序

Task 1

Learning Points

Listen to the following *words, phrases,* and *useful expressions* and read along. Then try to memorize them.

🔊 **Words and Phrases**

procedure	*n.*	程序
greet	*v.*	欢迎
fee	*n.*	费用
account	*n.*	账目，账户
input	*v.*	输入
incur	*v.*	发生（费用）
inquire	*v.*	询问，问明
extend	*v.*	转达，表达
in accordance with		与……一致
registration form		登记表

🔊 **Useful Expressions**

1. Asks the guest to show the room card or key card.
   请客人出示房卡或钥匙卡。
2. Prints out the bill and asks the guest to sign on the printed copy.
   打印账单，并请客人在打印单上签名。
3. Extends thanks to the guests for their stay and wishes them to visit the hotel again next time.
   对客人前来住店表示感谢，并期待他们再次光临。

Item 15 Checking Out

Task 2

🔊 Passage Reading

Listen to the short passage for the first time. Then practise it by reading it aloud by yourself.

Checkout Service Procedures

A. Greets the guest kindly when the guest comes to check out. **Asks the guest to show the room card or key card.**

B. Checks whether the room number on the room card is in accordance with the room number on the registration form.

C. Examines whether the fees incurred recently have been entered into an account.

D. Checks whether all the accounts have been input into the computer.

E. If there is no error after checking, **prints out the bill and asks the guest to sign on the printed copy.**

F. Inquires how the guest would like to pay and whether he/she has any special requirements. Checks out according to the different payment that the guest requires.

G. At the end of checkout, **extends thanks to the guests for their stay and wishes them to visit the hotel again in the future.**

Task 3

🔊 Listen and Answer

You will hear five questions. Listen carefully and give an appropriate answer to each of them.

(1) _____

(2) _____

(3) _____

(4) _____

(5) _____

Task 4

Oral Practice

Retell the text in your own words.

Task 5

More Oral and Listening Practice:
【Listening】Listen to the following dialogues and fill in the blanks.

🔊 Listening I

Exchanging Money

Cashier: Good afternoon! Can I help you?
Guest: Yes, I need to _____.
Cashier: What would you like?
Guest: What is _____ for the Euro?
Cashier: It's 1:7 to the Euro at the moment.
Guest: Well, I would like to change 500 Euros this time.
Cashier: Good. _____?
Guest: Yes. Here you are.
Cashier: Thank you. 500 Euros will be 3,500 yuan. _____
_____ and _____.
Guest: I'll take care of it. … Is that all right?
Cashier: Yes, here is _____ and _____.
Keep this _____.
Guest: Thank you for your help. Goodbye.
Cashier: Goodbye, Mr. Clarke. _____.

🔊 Listening II

A Mistake on the Hotel Bill

Staff: Can I help _____, please?
Guest: I'd like to check out, please.
Staff: _____, please?

Item 15 Checking Out

Guest:	Room 1408.
Staff:	One moment while I _____.
Guest:	Hmm, I thought the rate was 480 per night.
Staff:	Exactly, sir.
Guest:	What's this _____ of RMB _____?
Staff:	Oh, that's a 10 percent _____.
Guest:	Oh, OK. And this shows that I have a 108 _____. But I didn't use it.
Staff:	Oh, I'm terribly sorry. This must be a mistake. I'll _____ right away. Do you want to put your charges on your AMEX card?
Guest:	Yes. That's right.
Staff:	_____, please.
Guest:	Here you are.
Staff:	OK. Here's your copy, Mr. Smith. _____.

【Topics】Divide the class into groups. Choose one of the following topics to discuss in each group. Give a short report about the group's opinion afterward.

1. Do you think it is appropriate to severely punish a passenger who jokes about having a bomb? Why?

2. Does the last impression help to enhance the image of the tour guide? What should we do in order to establish a good impression for guests?

Item 16

Farewell, China 再见，中国

- **Model 1**
  See you Again Soon 再见

- **Model 2**
  Seeing Guests off at the Airport 机场送客

- **Model 3**
  A Farewell Speech 欢送词

Model 1
See you Again Soon 再见

Task 1

Warm-up

Work in pairs. Think about the following two topics and discuss with your partners.

1. Suppose you are an English tour guide now, how would you bid farewell to your guests? What would you say to them?
2. Do you think bidding farewell is of equal importance to the greetings? Why?

Task 2

Learning Points

Listen to the following *words, phrases,* and *useful expressions* and read along. Then try to memorize them.

🔊 Words and Phrases

coach	n.	旅游大巴车
accompany	v.	陪同
sincerely	adv.	真诚地
unforgettable	adj.	令人难忘的
comment	n.	评论
tour group		旅游团
more or less		或多或少
say goodbye (to)		向某人告别
all the way		全程
on behalf of …		代表……
sweet sorrow		喜忧参半

give sb. a big hand	喝彩

🔊 Useful Expressions

1. Your current visit to Shanghai is drawing to a close.
   大家的这次上海之行即将结束。
2. Even a good banquet has an end.
   天下没有不散的筵席。
3. I hope you have enjoyed your entire stay.
   希望你们在这里过得愉快。
4. Bon voyage!
   一路平安!
5. Could you fill out this form of evaluation for me?
   您能帮我填写一下评估表吗?
6. I'd like to express our heartfelt gratitude to you for your efforts and excellent services.
   对于你们所付出的努力和所提供的优质服务，我们表示衷心的感谢。

Task 3

🔊 Dialogue I

Listen to *Dialogue I* for the first time. Then practise the dialogue by reading it aloud with your partner. Read through it at least twice, changing your role each time.

See you Again Soon

【Scene】 *It is August 15. The tour group is getting on the coach and leaving for the airport in the morning.*

　　　　L: *Liu Hua (tour guide)*　　M: *Michael Wong (tour leader)*

L:　　Hello, Mr. Wong, ladies and gentlemen, **your current visit to Shanghai is drawing to a close.** I would like to say a few words before you leave. There is an old Chinese saying, **"Even a good banquet has an end."** I think you can more or less guess the meaning of it. I really hate to do this, but the time has come for us to say goodbye. It has been a wonderful experience for me to accompany you all the way. **I hope you have enjoyed your entire stay.** If there's anything that you are not satisfied with me, please do tell me so that I can do better in the future. And here, I'd like to take this opportunity to thank you all for your understanding, cooperation, and support. I hope to see you again in the future and to be your guide. I sincerely hope that you'll come to visit China again. **Bon voyage!**

G: Thank you, Miss Liu. You did a great job. We all had a very wonderful time. Let's give Miss Liu a big hand. (*Applause and cheers*)

L: Thank you. Before you leave, **could you fill out this form of evaluation for me?** The comments and suggestions that you provide will be very valuable to help plan future tours. (Liu Hua collects the forms.)

M: Thank you very much, Miss Liu. On behalf of the whole group, **I'd like to express our heartfelt gratitude to you for your efforts and excellent services.** We certainly have had a wonderful time in the past five days and will always remember this unforgettable journey. I believe, there will be further cooperation between us.

L: I suppose we have to part. Parting is such sweet sorrow. Hope to meet you again. Have a pleasant trip!

M: Thank you!

Task 4

🔊 Listen and Answer

You will hear five questions. Listen carefully and give an appropriate answer to each of them.

(1) _____

(2) _____

(3) _____

(4) _____

(5) _____

Task 5

Role-play

Act out the following dialogues.

Item 16 Farewell, China

【Situation A】 A tour guide is bidding farewell to a tour group who are leaving for their country. Before the guests leave, there are a large number of matters a tour guide must attend to:

☆ Asks the bellman to collect together the baggage which needs checking.

☆ Checks the amount of the baggage and whether they are locked or damaged with the tour leader.

☆ Helps the tourists to check out, reminds them to take their own items including their travel certificates, and warns them to take care of their valuables.

☆ Asks the tourists to check whether there is something for the local guide to deal with for them after their departure.

☆ Stands beside the door of the coach and assists the tourists to get on.

☆ Counts the number of the tourists again, confirms that no tourists' items are forgotten, then asks the driver to start.

【Situation B】 British Tour is now on the way to the airport. The tour guide is now bidding farewell to her guests. They all feel regretful at parting because they all had a memorable experience.

Model 2
Seeing Guests off at the Airport　机场送客

Task 1

Warm-up

Work in pairs. Learn the following words and answer the questions below.

reconfirm	air ticket	Information Office	departure time	air flight
check-in desk	in advance	boarding card/pass	luggage claim card	

What are the procedure for checking in at the airport?

Task 2

Learning Points

Listen to the following *words, phrases,* and *useful expressions* and read along. Then try to memorize them.

🔊 **Words and Phrases**

cart	n.	手推车
lobby	n.	大厅
interpret	v.	讲解
boarding pass		登机牌
luggage claim card		行李牌
security-check		安全检查
group visa		团队签证

🔊 Useful Expressions

1. Here we are at the airport.
   现在我们到达机场了。
2. Would you please wait for me for a few seconds?
   请等我几分钟好吗?
3. Take your time.
   慢慢来。
4. It's time for us to say goodbye to each other.
   到了我们相互道别的时候了。
5. Thank you for all your kindness.
   感谢您的好心。
6. Hope to see you soon.
   希望能再次见到您。
7. A happy journey home.
   回家旅途愉快。

Task 3

🔊 Dialogue II

Listen to the *dialogue II* for the first time. Then practise the dialogue by reading it aloud with your partner. Read through it at least twice, changing your role each time.

Seeing Guests off at the Airport

【Scene】 *Now the tour group has gotten off the coach, and the guests arrive at the gate of the airport.*

    J: Janet Jin (tour guide) D: Daniel Black (tour leader)

  J: **Here we are at the airport.** I will get some carts to carry your baggage.
  D: Let me go with you.

【Scene】 *They return with the carts, put the suitcases on carts, and push them to the lobby of the airport ... Now, they are inside the Airport Departure Lounge.*

  J: **Would you please wait for me for a few seconds?** I am going to get the boarding passes and luggage claim cards for you!
  D: OK, **take your time**.

【Scene】 *The tour guide comes back. ...Now, it's time for them to say goodbye to each other.*

J: Thank you for your waiting. Here are your tickets, boarding passes, and luggage claim cards. Please check them.

D: Thank you very much.

J: Shall we go for the security-check now?

D: OK. Let's go.

J: Please get your plane ticket, group visa, and boarding pass ready.

D: Thanks for your help.

J: It's my pleasure.

D: Well, Miss Jin, **it's time for us to say goodbye to each other.**

J: Yes, I suppose we must. I have enjoyed all these days you have spent with us, and I'll always remember them. **Thank you for all your kindness.**

D: I have enjoyed your interpreting. You have done a wonderful job. I hope you'll be my guide again next time I'm here.

J: I hope so, too.

D: Goodbye, Miss Jin. **Hope to see you soon.**

J: Goodbye. **A happy journey home**, and hope to see you again soon.

Task 4

🔊 Listen and Answer

You will hear five questions. Listen carefully and give an appropriate answer to each of them.

(1) _____

(2) _____

(3) _____

(4) _____

(5) _____

Task 5

Role-play

Act out the following dialogues.

Item 16 Farewell, China

【Situation A】 You are an English tour guide who is saying goodbye to an American tourist at the airport. Mr. Davidson is the tourist.

Tour guide:
☆ Asks to gather the baggage.
☆ Helps check in.
☆ Reminds Mr. Davidson to keep his passport, credit card, and travelers check handy for the security check.
☆ Tells that the airport tax is included in the air ticket.
☆ Expresses great honor to serve Mr. Davidson.
☆ Hopes that Mr. Davidson enjoys his trip home.
☆ Welcomes him to China again.

Mr. Davidson:
☆ Thanks the guide for accompanying him to the airport.
☆ Asks about the airport tax.
☆ Thanks for all that has been done for him.
☆ Appreciates every minute of his stay here.
☆ Wishes everything goes well.

【Situation B】 The tourists are checking in at the airport with the local guide. With his help, the tourists go through the formalities required. Then they bid farewell at the security check.

Model 3
A Farewell Speech 欢送词

Task 1

Learning Points

Listen to the following *words, phrases,* and *useful expressions* and read along. Then try to memorize them.

🔊 **Words and Phrases**

opportunity	n.	机会
promote	v.	促进
patience	n.	耐心
cooperation	n.	合作
satisfy	v.	满意
Confucius	n.	孔子
build up		建立
Fenghua Honey Peach		奉化水蜜桃
Qianceng Cookie		千层饼

🔊 **Useful Expressions**

1. Your trip to Ningbo is drawing to a close.
   你们来宁波的行程即将结束。
2. During these ten days, you have visited most of the famous scenic spots in Ningbo.
   在这10天当中,你们游览了宁波大多数的著名景点。
3. All this will certainly promote your understanding of the economic and social development of Ningbo.
   这些经历都将帮助你们理解宁波的经济和社会的发展。
4. We would like to thank you again for your great patience, cooperation, and understanding.

我们要再次感谢各位给予的耐心、合作和理解。

5. The tour couldn't have been as successful without your support.
   要不是你们的支持，这次旅游不可能这么成功。

6. If there's anything that you are not satisfied with about us, please do tell us.
   如果你们有什么不满意，请务必告诉我们。

7. We sincerely hope that you'll come to visit Ningbo again.
   我们诚挚地希望你们再来宁波旅游。

8. There is nothing more delightful than to meet friends from afar.
   有朋自远方来，不亦乐乎。

9. Please send my best regards to your families, your relatives, and your friends.
   请将我最好的祝福带给你们的亲朋好友。

10. I wish every one of you a good journey home.
    希望你们每一个人回程愉快。

Task 2

Passage Reading

Listen to the short passage for the first time. Then practise it by reading it aloud by yourself.

A Farewell Speech

Hello, my dear guests. After over ten days, **your trip to Ningbo is drawing to a close**. You will leave Ningbo for America tomorrow morning. At this moment, please allow me to take this opportunity to say something on behalf of our Youth Travel Service.

First of all, we thank you for coming. This trip is long enough for us to build up our friendship. **During these ten days, you have visited most of the famous scenic spots in Ningbo,** such as Xikou Scenic Area, Tianyi Pavilion, and Dongqian Lake. You have touched mysterious but charming Chinese culture and tasted delicious food, such as Fenghua Honey Peach and Xikou Qianceng Cookie. **All this will certainly promote your understanding of the economic and social development of Ningbo.**

Secondly, **we would like to thank you again for your great patience, cooperation, and understanding,** which have made our job easier. **The tour couldn't have been as successful without your support.**

Thirdly, **if there's anything that you are not satisfied with about us, please do tell us** so that we can do better in the future.

Lastly, **we sincerely hope that you'll come to visit Ningbo again.** Confucius, the greatest teacher in Chinese history, said that **"there is nothing more delightful than to meet friends from afar"**. I believe that our friendship will grow fast and I would like to welcome you back. Upon your return to America, **please send my best regards to your families, your relatives, and your friends.** And **I wish every one of you a good journey home.** Thank you!

Task 3

🔊 Listen and Answer

You will hear five questions. Listen carefully and give an appropriate answer to each of them.

(1) _____

(2) _____

(3) _____

(4) _____

(5) _____

Task 4

Oral Practice

Make a "Farewell Speech" with your partner. You should mention all the key points.

Task 5

More Oral and Listening Practice:

【Listening】 Listen to the dialogues and fill in the blanks.

🔊 Listening I

Check-in at the Train Station

A: _____?

B: Yes, let's go on board to avoid the last-minute rush.
A: _____.
OK. Let's move on to the ticket control.
B: Where is the ticket control for going to Hangzhou?
A: Over there, at Gate 3. _____ and wait to get them punched.
B: To which platform are we going?
A: Platform 3. _____.
B: Thank you.
A: Here we are. Platform 3. The car is just ahead. Car 6. Please get on.
B: It's a nice car. My seat is there.
A: _____, on the rack or under the seat?
B: On the rack, please. Thank you.
A: Good. _____?
B: No, thank you. You have been a great help. Thank you, indeed.
A: It's my pleasure. The train starts in a few minutes. Now it's time for us to say goodbye. _____.
B: Goodbye, Mr. Guide. Thank you for your help.

Listening II

Seeing Guests Off

G: guide   T: tourists

G: Is everything in order now?
T1: Yes. _____?
G: At eleven thirty. There is still half an hour to go. _____.
T2: Mr. Hu, during our trip in the past ten days, you've shown your concern for us in every respect. I really don't know how to express my gratitude.
G: _____.
T1: Before I came here, I only had an understanding of China from books, papers, television and films. Now I've seen China with my own eyes.
G: _____.
T1: It's a pity we haven't had enough time for many other places.
G: _____. You're always welcome.
T1: Wonderful. I hope we'll keep in touch.

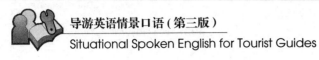

G: _____.
T2: Goodbye, Mr. Hu. Thank you very much.
G: _____!

【Topics】Divide the class into groups. Choose one of the following topics to discuss in each group. Give a short report about the group's opinion after that.

1. Many Chinese people including many students have experienced refusals of their visa application. What do you think are the most common reasons?

2. What can you do to make sure that you have made your guests satisfied?

3. The Yellow River has become an elevated river in the lower reaches, threatening to cause destruction. Do you have any suggestions as to the solution to the problem?

Appendix 1
The Eight Different Cooking Styles in China
中国八大菜系

Sichuan Style 川菜
Pork shreds with fishy flavour 鱼香肉丝
Tofu with mince and chilli oil 麻婆豆腐
Diced chicken with chilli pepper 宫保鸡丁
Stewed scallop and turnip ball 绣球干贝
Steamed pork wrapped in lotus leaves 荷叶蒸肉
Translucent beef slices 灯影牛肉
Spicy Sichuan-style tender chicken slices 怪味鸡块
Shrimp with green vegetables 翡翠虾仁

Shandong Style 鲁菜
Dezhou grilled chicken 德州扒鸡
Chinese yam in hot toffee 拔丝山药
Quick-boiled clam 油爆大蛤
Lotus flower and shrimp 荷花大虾
Bird's nest in clear soup 清汤燕窝
Braised sea whelks in brown sauce 红烧海螺
Braised sea slug with crab meat in brown sauce 蟹烧海参

Guangdong Style 粤菜
Stewed crab meat and eggplant 虾肉烧茄子
Stuffed duck shaped as gourd 八珍葫芦鸭
Crisp-skinned chicken 脆皮鸡
Sliced chicken with oyster sauce 蚝油滑鸡片
Roasted suckling pig 烤乳猪
Shark's fin with crab ovum 虾黄鱼翅
Sweet-sour pork fillet with chilli 糖醋咕噜肉

Huaiyang Style 淮扬菜

Chicken mousse broth with fresh corn 鸡茸玉米
Yincai vegetables cooked with chicken slices 银菜鸡丝
Scallop wrapped in chicken breast slices 鸡片包干贝
Squid with crispy rice crust 鱿鱼锅巴
Crab meat & minced pork ball in casserole 蟹粉狮子头

Fujian Cuisine 闽菜

Sea food and poultry in casserole 佛跳墙
Steamed chicken ball with egg white 蒸芙蓉鸡球
Fried prawn shaped as a pair of fish 太极明虾
Saute shredded whelks in rice wine sauce 炝糟响螺
Steamed pork roll with rice flour and lotus leaf 荷叶米粉肉
Crisp pomfret with litchi 荔枝鲳鱼

Hunan Cuisine 湘菜

Steamed turtle 清蒸甲鱼
White bait in chafing dish 银鱼火锅
Braised shark's fin in brown sauce 红煨鱼翅
Sweet lotus seed 冰糖湘莲
Braised dried pork with eel slices 腊肉焖鳝片
Crispy rice crust with sea cucumber 锅巴海参
Spring chicken with cayenne pepper 麻辣仔鸡

Anhui Cuisine 徽菜

Huangshan stewed pigeon 黄山炖鸽
Gourd duck 葫芦鸭子
Fricassee pork sinew with egg white 芙蓉蹄筋
Crispy pork with pine nuts 松子米酥肉
Spicy fried chicken 椒盐米鸡

Zhejiang Food 浙江菜

West Lake vinegar fish 西湖醋鱼
Shelled shrimps with Dragon Well tea leaves 龙井虾仁
West Lake water shied soup 西湖莼菜汤
Eight-jewel rice pudding wrapped with lotus leaves 八宝荷叶饭
Beggar's chicken 叫花鸡
Dongpo Pork 东坡肉

Appendix 2
Listening material 听力材料

Item 1 Meeting Guests

Model 1: Meeting Guests at the Airport

  TASK4 Listen and Answer

  1. Are you Mr. Green from Los Angeles?
  2. Did you have a good trip?
  3. Is everyone in the group here?
  4. Shall I help you with your luggage?
  5. Is the shuttle bus waiting outside?

Model 2: A Welcome Speech

  TASK4   Listen and Answer

  1. Which city do the tourists visit?
  2. What's the guide's name?
  3. Which travel service is the guide from?
  4. Who is the driver?
  5. How many years of driving experience does the driver have?

Model 3: On the Way to the Hotel

  TASK4   Listen and Answer

  1. Are there any famous scenic spots in Ningbo?
  2. What are the three rivers?
  3. Where is the hometown of Mr. Chiang Kai-shek?
  4. What's the name of the big square?
  5. Where is the hotel located?

Model 4:   China—a Country with an Ancient Civilization

  TASK3 Listen and Answer

  1. Does China have a written history of over 5,000 years of civilization?
  2. What are the China's rich tourist resources? Please give some examples.

3. What are the Four Great Inventions?
4. Where is the capital city of the People's Republic of China?
5. How many years of contemporary history does Beijing have?

TASK5 More Oral and Listening Practice
Listening I

At the Airport

A: Excuse me, but are you Mr. Davis from the UK?
B: Why, yes, I'm Mark Davis.
A: Oh, Mr. Davis. I'm very glad to meet you. My name is Zhu Lan. I'm the guide from the Beijing Travel Service.
B: Hello, Ms Zhu. Thank you for coming to meet us.
A: Welcome to China Mr. Davis. How was your trip?
B: Fine. We had a very pleasant flight. Let me introduce you to Miss Tyler, my assistant. She is in charge of the daily affairs of our tour group.
A: How do you do, Miss Tyler? I'm pleased to meet you.
C: How do you do? I'm pleased to meet you, too.
A: We've made reservations for your party at the Hong Kong Garden Hotel.
C: Thank you very much.
A: Shall we go to the hotel now? The shuttle bus is just waiting outside.
C: Fine.
A: Your luggage will be sent to your rooms in the hotel.
C: That's good.
A: May I help with your suitcase, Mr. Davis?
B: It's very kind of you.

Listening II

Traveling in Beijing

There are many fascinating sights in and __near__ Beijing, but before visiting the attractions, spend an hour or two walking the streets. __Get__ off the main boulevards and wander through the maze-like alleys where __most__ residents live or perhaps stroll down Old Culture Street. If your hotel is downtown, walk to the walled 14th-century Forbidden City, so __named__ because it was off limits to ordinary citizens. On its grounds are six palaces and 800 smaller buildings, containing __9000__ rooms. The main gate of the palace opens onto Tian'anmen Square. The square is the site of the Monument to the People's Heroes, Chairman Mao Zedong Memorial Hall, the Great Hall of the People, the Museum of Chinese History, and the Museum of the Chinese Revolution.

Appendix 2 Listening material

Item 2 Hotel Check-in

Model 1: Hotel Room Reservation

TASK4   Listen and Answer

1. Who is the caller, where is he from?
2. How long would the visitor stay in the hotel?
3. What kind of room would the visitor like to reserve?
4. What is the price to stay at the hotel for three days?
5. Is it possible to have some discount?

Model 2: Checking in

TASK4   Listen and Answer

1. What is the name of the tourist group?
2. How many rooms has the group reserved?
3. What is the name of the travel agency that reserved the rooms for the group?
4. How long will the group stay in the hotel?
5. What time is breakfast served in the hotel?

Model 3: Itinerary Planning

TASK4   Listen and Answer

1. How long will the tour last?
2. Where will the tourists have lunch on the first day?
3. Where will the tourists visit on the second day?
4. Is there some extra cost for detour?
5. What should the tourist bring tomorrow?

Model 4: Process of Hotel Guest Registration

TASK3   Listen and Answer

1. When greeting a guest, what should you pay attention to?
2. When addressing a guest, what title can you use?
3. Upon receiving the credit card, what information should you check?
4. What should be done with the credit card?
5. What information should be checked before giving the guest the room key?

TASK5   More Oral and Listening Practice
Listening I

A Group Reservation

R: Good morning. Reservations. <u>How can I help you</u>?

C: Good morning. I'd like to reserve rooms for my group.

R: What type of rooms do you want to reserve?

C: We have 10 people. Five twin rooms, please.

R: For which dates?

C: From 21st to 23rd of March.

R: Wait a minute, please. Five twin rooms for March from 21st to 23rd. Yes, those rooms are available.

C: What will be the rate?

R: It's 600 RMB per night.

C: Can you give us a special rate since we always stay in your hotel?

R: May I have your name, please?

C: Brutes Lewis from General Traveling Company.

R: Oh, Yes, Mr. Lewis, there is a 20 percent discount for regular customers.

C: How can I guarantee my reservation?

R: You can guarantee the reservation with your credit card number.

C: My Visa card number is 3600 54762 5819.

R: OK. Mr. Lewis. How will you be arriving?

C: By air. Do you have pick-up service?

R: When will you be arriving at the airport?

C: The arrival time should be 12:45.

R: OK. Our hotel bus will be there at that time.

Listening II

Extending the Stay

R: Good morning, sir. May I help you?

G: I meant to check out today, but I have to stay three more nights here.

R: May I know your name and room number, please?

G: Andrew Stowe of Room 618.

R: Please wait a minute, Mr. Stowe. I'll check the computer record. Here, today is 12th. You want to extend your stay till 15th?

G: Yes, exactly.

R: I'm sorry, sir. You can only stay in that room for one more night. Your floor was reserved for a conference from the 14th.

G: What will be my next two nights?

R: Would you mind changing to room 819?

C: Not at all.

R: Thank you, sir. This is your registration form. Please change the departure date with the 15th.

G: OK.

Item 3 Housekeeping Service

Model 1: Escorting the Guest into the Guest Room

TASK4   Listen and Answer

1. What is the room number of Mr. Jones?
2. Is Jones satisfied with the size of the room?
3. What is an IDD call, how to make an IDD call in the room?
4. Is the Internet available in the room, how much is it?
5. Where should the valuables be kept?

Model 2: Making up the Room

TASK4 Listen and Answer:

1. When will the Browns want to have their turn-down service?
2. Who will do the turn-down service for the Browns?
3. What is the room attendant required to do now?
4. What will Mr. Brown do while waiting for the friends?
5. Are the Browns satisfied with the room attendant?

Model 3: About Room Service Order

TASK4 Listen and Answer

1. Why does Mr. Lock make the phone call?
2. What did Mr. Lock order for the breakfast?
3. How much more does a pot cost than a cup of coffee?
4. How long should Mr. Lock wait for the breakfast?
5. What is the room number of Mr. Lock?

Model 4: Hotels Today

TASK3   Listen and Answer

1. What are the two main groups of hotels?
2. Where are the resort hotels located?
3. What is a residential hotel?
4. Where are the inns and hotels located?
5. How much will a double room in a moderate hotel cost a day?

TASK5   More Oral and Listening Practice
Listening I

A Morning Call

A: Can I help you, sir?
B: It's <u>my first visit</u> here. Do you have <u>morning call</u> service?

A: Yes, would you like to have it?

B: Yes, I want to _have it_ tomorrow morning.

A: _What time_ do you want to have it?

B: At _6:30_ tomorrow morning. I want to get up early so that I can watch people playing Chinese boxing.

A: Oh, I see. What kind of call would you like, by phone or _knocking at the door_?

B: By phone, I don't like to disturb my neighbors.

A: Your room number, please.

B: _918_.

A: OK, sir. Our _room attendant_ will do that for you.

Listening II

Cleaning the Room

A: Housekeeping. May I _come in_?

B: Yes, please.

A: Good morning, sir. May I clean the room now?

B: No, not so far. Thanks. I'm not feeling very well now. I've _got a cold_.

A: Oh, I'm sorry to hear that. Shall I _call the doctor_?

B: Not necessary. I've got some medicine.

A: Would you like some boiled water?

B: Yes, please switch on the mini jar to make me some boiled water.

A: Yes, sir. May I replace the bed sheet and toilet needs?

B: That's very kind of you.

A: Should I turn on the "Don't disturb" light?

B: Yes, please. I want to have a good rest.

Item 4 Food & Beverage Service

Model 1: Reserving a Table

TASK4 Listen and Answer

1. What is the name of the restaurant?

2. What time is the table reserved for?

3. How many of the people would come for the table reserved?

4. Which room is reserved for the customer?

5. Does the customer have a dress code?

Model 2: Food & Beverage Service

TASK4 Listen and Answer

1. What's the name of the hotel?

Appendix 2 Listening material

2. When will the tourist group have lunch?

3. Are there vegetarians in the group?

4. What is the hotel famous for?

5. Where can the tourist group have a rest after meals?

Model 3: The Payment

TASK4 Listen and Answer

1. What is the total of the bill?

2. How much is it in US dollars?

3. How would the customer pay the bill?

4. What credit cards does the customer have?

5. What is the exchange rate that day?

Model 4: The Chinese Food

TASK3 Listen and Answer

1. What are the four words used to describe Chinese food?

2. What are the four regional cuisine that are recognized without dispute in China?

3. What are the characteristics of Sichuan cuisine?

4. What are the features of Shandong cuisine?

5. Is an average Chinese home meal different from that of the banquet?

TASK5 More Oral and Listening Practice
Listening I

Breakfast

W: Good morning sir and madam. What would you like to have?

M1: <u>What do you serve</u> for breakfast?

W: We serve <u>Continental</u> and <u>American</u> breakfast.

M1: What do you serve for <u>Continental</u> breakfast?

W: We serve rolls with <u>butter and coffee</u>.

M1: What about <u>American</u> breakfast?

W: Orange or <u>tomato</u> juice, tea or <u>coffee</u>, toast with butter or jam, and <u>eggs</u> with bacon.

M1: I'll have <u>tomato</u> juice, <u>tea</u>, and two eggs. Can I have <u>ham</u> instead of bacon?

W: Certainly, madam. And you, sir?

M2: I'll have <u>the same as</u> my wife.

Listening II

At a Chinese Restaurant

W: Good evening, sir. Can I help you?

G: I'd like to <u>try some Chinese food</u>, but <u>I have no idea</u> about Chinese food. Can you give me some suggestions?

W: Well, there are different styles of cuisine.
G: Can you give me some more information?
W: Four styles of food are especially known throughout China. They are Shandong, Cantonese, Sichuan, and Huaiyang.
G: What is the Cantonese food like?
W: It is lighter and fresh.
G: How about Shandong food?
W: It's spicy and heavy.
G: And what about the Huaiyang food?
W: It's famous for its sweet flavor.
G: The last one, Sichuan food is?
W: Sichuan dishes are hot and pungent.
G: Oh, really? I like hot food. What do you recommend?
W: The famous Sichuan dishes are Mapo bean curd and shredded meat in chili sauce.
G: I'll have them.

Item 5 City Sightseeing and Transportation

Model 1: City Tours

TASK4 Listen and Answer

1. Which city in China is the Oriental Manhattan?
2. What are these buildings of European architectural styles known as?
3. Who built these buildings?
4. What's the name of the TV tower?
5. How high is it?

Model 2: Car Rental Service

TASK4 Listen and Answer

1. What does the tourist want to do?
2. Why does the tourist want to rent a car?
3. What's the first procedure of renting a car?
4. Which German cars can be found in the car rental company?
5. How much deposit does the tourist have to pay for the car?

Model 3: Xikou

TASK3 Listen and Answer

1. What's the population of Xikou?
2. Which is the former residence of Chiang Kai-shek?
3. Where is the Fenggao House located?

4. Which stream is in front of the Fenggao House?

5. What does its construction pattern consist of?

TASK5 More Oral and Listening Practice
Listening I

On the Plane

A: Ladies and gentlemen, now we're on the plane to New York, first you should find your seats and place your luggage in order. If you have any questions, you can ask me.

B: Hello, can you show me where my seat is?

A: Of course. 20A. That will be four rows up on the right. It's a window seat.

B: Thank you. By the way, where can I put my bag?

A: You may place it under your seat or in the overhead compartment.

B: Like this?

A: Yes, that's fine.

B: What are all these buttons and plugs in the arm rest?

A: Well, this one is the seat-recliner button. If you push the button, the seat of your chair slides out and the back reclines so you can relax and be comfortable. But for take-off and landing, the seat must be in an upright position.

B: And this one?

A: Wait. Don't push that. That's call button. If you need the stewardess for anything, you push that button which turns on a light near where she works and she'll come to see what you need.

B: Oh, I see.

A: Sir, please don't smoke until we are airborne and the "No Smoking" sign is turned off.

B: Oh, sorry.

A: Also please make certain that your seat belt is securely fastened and your seat is in the upright position.

B: OK. Thank you.

Listening II

Ningbo

As an old cultural city with a clear distinction of four seasons and moderate climate, Ningbo has nurtured many talented people. There are 225 cultural relics in Ningbo, among which the Hemudu Cultural Relics have a history of 7000 years. The Tianyi Building is the oldest book-collecting building in China. The Baoguo temple is the oldest wooden one on the upper reaches of Yangzi River. The Yue Kiln in Shanglin is one of the origins of Chinese civilization. The ancient irrigation works in Tashanyan together with the former residence of Chiang kai-shek are both important cultural relics under national preservation. Besides,

Tiantong temple is the No. 2 temple to advocate Zen Sect. The Ayuwang Temple has in it the mummy of Sakyamuni. The Xuedou Temple is a <u>Buddhist</u> rite of Maitreya and a resort where people pay respect to Buddhism. The Dongqian Lake is the biggest <u>freshwater</u> lake in Zhejiang province. These <u>scenic spots</u>, together with Putuo Mountains on its east, Yandang Mountains on its south, West Lake on its west, and Shanghai on its north, are sure to make Ningbo a nice place for <u>tourists</u> from all over the world.

Item 6 The Service of Travel Destinations

Model 1: Narrations on Tour

TASK4 Listen and Answer

1. Where are they going?
2. How long will the tour last?
3. What is their evening schedule?
4. When was the Great Wall enlisted in the World Cultural Heritage by UNESCO?
5. When will they assemble?

Model 2: At the Ticket Box

TASK4 Listen and Answer

1. Where is the hometown of Lu Xun?
2. What dose the package include?
3. What can the tourist expect to see at these places?
4. Are the program schedule and map free?
5. How much is each ticket?

Model 3: Asking the Way

TASK4 Listen and Answer

1. Is the Baoguo Temple very far?
2. Which bus could the tourist take?
3. Where is the bus station?
4. Where's the subway station?
5. How long does it take the tourist to get there?

Model 4: The Role of a Tour Guide

TASK3 Listen and Answer

1. What's the first duty of a guide?
2. What should the guide pay particular attention to?
3. Should the guide supervise the transporting of the tour members' luggage?
4. What should the guide do if a tour member needs a double room on his/her own?

5. With whom should the guide coordinate all arrangements in cooperation?

TASK5 More Oral and Listening Practice
Listening I

How to get to People's Square?

T: Excuse me, <u>how long does it take to get to People's Square</u>?
S: By subway or by bus?
T: <u>Which would you recommend</u>?
S: At this time of day, <u>it is definitely faster to take the subway</u>. It takes about 10 to 20 minutes. <u>Would you like directions</u>?
T: That would be most helpful. Thanks.
S: Sure, my pleasure. <u>The nearest station is very close</u>, right on the corner of Huaihai Road. You will see the signs with a red "H". Take <u>the metro line 1 going east. It's just two stops to</u> the People's Square Station.
T: <u>You're very helpful</u>. Thank you.
S: You're welcome. Hope you will enjoy your day.

Listening II

The Global Concept of Tour Guide Service

The global <u>concept</u> of tour guide service <u>contains</u> 7 meanings represented by the word "SERVICE" with 7 letters.

S: It is "smile", the tour guide should <u>provide</u> smiling service.
E: Excellent. Service should be <u>performed</u> in an excellent way.
R: Ready. The tour guide is constantly <u>ready</u> to serve tourists.
V: Viewing. Each tourist should be <u>treated</u> as a <u>distinguished</u> guest requiring his or her <u>special</u> care.
I: Inviting. Tourists will be invited to <u>return</u> after he/she leaves the city or the country.
C: Creating. The tour guide should create an amiable and <u>harmonious</u> environment for tourists.
E: Eye. Each tour guide pays a close <u>attention</u> to tourists with keen <u>observation</u>, anticipates their needs and provides his or her service in time which makes tourists feel that they are <u>carefully</u> and constantly <u>concerned</u> by the tour guide.

Item 7 Tour of Gardens

Model 1: A Trip to the Yuyuan Garden

TASK4 Listen and Answer

1. Why does Jack invite Miss Zhang to travel to Yuyuan Garden?

2. What usually attracts most tourists when they visit Yuyuan Garden?

3. When and why did Pan Yunduan build Yuyuan Garden?

4. How many scenes are there in the garden?

5. Which two scenes are mentioned in detail in the dialogue?

Model 2: Touring the Summer Palace

TASK4 Listen and Answer

1. Of which type of garden is the Summer Palace?

2. What functions does the peculiar animal have?

3. What can they see when they reach the top of the Longevity Hill?

4. How much does Kunming Lake take up the Summer Palace?

5. What other tour attractions will they visit after a short rest?

Model 3: The Four Elements in a Traditional Garden

TASK4 Listen and Answer

1. What is a general feature of Chinese classical garden architecture?

2. What are the four elements of a Chinese garden?

3. What features of rocks attract a garden designer?

4. Why is water considered as the central element of a garden?

5. What kind of principles would a garden designer follow when he designed a classical garden?

Model 4: Suzhou Gardens

TASK3 Listen and Answer

1. What is Suzhou renowned as?

2. What are the four classical gardens in China?

3. What are the four classical gardens in Suzhou?

4. Among the gardens in Suzhou, which one is the largest?

5. Which garden is also called a "Kingdom of Rockeries"?

TASK 5 More Oral and Listening Practice:
Listening I

Touring the Grand View Garden

A:　　Today we are going to visit the famous Grand View Garden. Our bus will stop at a small bridge and we'll climb the nearby tower to <u>have a bird's-eye view of</u> the Grand View Garden. <u>Now we're on the top.</u> Look at these buildings with white walls and black roofs.

B:　　<u>What a beautiful garden!</u>

A:　　Yes, it is a typical garden in the south of the Yangtze River. Now we'd like to see a screen wall.

Appendix 2 Listening material

B: Are we going to the main entrance to the Garden?
A: Yes, but we have to go around the screen wall.
B: Aha, why does the screen wall stand in the way?
A: It protects the privacy of those inside. And it also makes it more difficult for evil spirits to enter.
B: I see.
A: Have you ever visited such places before?
B: No. I've never been to these places in China before.
A: Now we will walk through the heavy red gate and into the courtyards with unique styles. Just ahead, there is a group of strange rocks, ponds, and willows. Among them is the home of Jia Baoyu, one major character of *The Story of Stones* by Cao Xueqin.
B: What a peaceful and romantic sight!

Listening II

Visiting the Chengde Mountain Summer Resort

A: It is said that the Chengde Mountain Summer Resort is the largest surviving imperial garden complex in China. It is even a lot bigger than the Summer Palace in Beijing. Is that true?
B: Yes, it covers an area of 5.6million square meters which is about twice the size of the Summer Palace. And the mountain resort consists of a palace area and a scenery area. Which part should we visit first?
A: Let's tour the scenery area first since we have visited many palaces in Beijing. The palaces here are mostly made from dark hardwood. In the scenery area, there is a big lake. Lotuses and pines grow around.
B: OK. Let's go around the scenery area first. Look, the scenery area here has great charm, reminding one of the land south of the Yangtze River. And the water in the lake is so clear and blue.
A: The hill over there is called Gold Hill. It is surrounded by the lake on three sides. Standing on the top of the hill, you can enjoy a very good view of the beautiful lake scenery. Is there a spring flowing out of the cracks in the north of the Gold Hill?
B: Yes. It is called the Warm River Spring.
A: Oh, look at the peak on the east.
B: It looks like an inverted washing club, so people call it the Club Peak（棒槌峰）. It's so unique.
A: The view is really magnificent. This kind of beautiful scenery is rare in the north of China. I feel as if I were in a different world.
B: Why don't we take some pictures here?
A: That's a good idea.

Item 8 Tour of Mountains

Model 1: In Huangshan

TASK4 Listen and Answer

1. What is Mount Huangshan also called?

2. What are the four wonders of Mount Huangshan?

3. Can you list two famous odd pines in Mount Huangshan?

4. What functions do hot springs have?

5. Does Mount Huangshan deserve "No. 1 Mountain under Heaven"?

Model 2: A Trip in Guilin

TASK4 Listen and Answer

1. When people talk about Guilin, which sentence is generally used to describe it?

2. What are the "Four Wonders" of Guilin's landscape?

3. Can you list three scenic areas in Guilin?

4. How can you describe the water in the Lijiang River?

5. What is the tourist's comment on the Elephant Trunk Hill?

Model 3: Huangguoshu Waterfall

TASK4 Listen and Answer

1. What are the width and the length of the Huangguoshu Waterfall?

2. Among dozens of waterfalls, which fall is the biggest in Asia?

3. Where can tourists touch the flying water with hands and see the falls from different angles?

4. What is the rainbow like on a sunny day?

5. What do you think of the scene when the waterfall pours into the Xiniu Pool spectacularly?

Model 4: West Lake

TASK3 Listen and Answer

1. What is the famous saying which is usually used to describe Hangzhou?

2. For which is Hangzhou famous?

3. How many sections do the Sue Causeway and the Bai Causeway divide the West Lake into?

4. Can you list the four islands of the West Lake?

5. Could you list half of the top ten famous scenic spots of the West Lake designated in the South Song Dynasty?

Appendix 2 Listening material

TASK5 More Oral and Listening Practice

Listening I

Touring Guilin

Guilin is primarily known for its charming and unique scenery. It has always been considered as __China's most beautiful scenery__. Many Chinese poets and painters, both __ancient and modern__, have been drawn to it, and they have all praised the beauty of Guilin __in their works__.

Guilin offers tourists __a number of interesting sights__. Hills of Guilin are unique, which have been attracting __and astonishing visitors__ from all over the world __for many centuries__. The hills have fantastically shaped peaks, studded with pines and small pavilions. So the landscape of Guilin has been praised as __the best under heaven__.

Listening II

Mount Lushan

Located in the northern part of Jiangxi Province, Mount Lushan faces the Yangtze River to the north and borders on the east with __the largest fresh water lake__ in China, Poyang Lake. The mountain consists of __99 peaks__, the tallest being Dahanyang, rising to the height of __1,474 meters__ above sea level. Altogether there are __474 scenic spots__ in twelve scenic areas. The beauty of Lushan Mountain is attributed to its exotic peaks and mysterious caves, thunderous waterfalls and gurgling springs, ancient temples and stone forest, and buildings that seem to be suspended in midair. With this fantastic blend of mountains, water, and cliffs, Mount Lushan is one of China's best summer resorts. Its beauty has been admired for centuries. About __1,200 years ago__, Li Bai, a master poet of the Tang Dynasty, portrayed Mount Lushan in his poems, paying homage to the magnificent scenery he saw and enjoyed. He used this area as inspiration for many of his over __900 poems__. In 1996 Mount Lushan was listed as __a world cultural heritage site__.

Item 9 Tour of Temples

Model 1: Visiting the Jade Buddha Temple

TASK4 Listen and Answer

1. When was the Jade Buddha Temple constructed?
2. For what was the Jade Buddha Temple set up?
3. Who brought the two jade Buddha statues to Shanghai?
4. How many major buildings are there in the Jade Buddha Temple? What are they?
5. Where are the two jade Buddhas worshipped?

Model 2: Visiting the Confucius Temple

TASK4 Listen and Answer

1. What is Qufu famous for?

2. What are the three attractions concerning Confucius in Qufu?

3. In the Temple of Confucius, which building is the highest and the most important?

4. Can you name the place where Confucius gave his lectures in his later years?

5. How many students did Confucius have in his life?

Model 3: Visiting the Wudang Mountain

TASK3 Listen and Answer:

1. What is the height of the Tianzhu Peak?

2. What is the Wudang Mountain renowned for?

3. When was the ancient building complex of the Wudang Mountain listed as the World Cultural Heritage?

4. What is your comment on the Golden Hall on the Tianzhu Peak?

5. How about the Daoist music in the Wudang Mountain?

TASK5 More Oral and Listening Practice:

Listening I

Visiting the Jinshan Temple

A: Ladies and gentlemen, now we are at the main entrance to the Jinshan Temple.

B: <u>Most of your temples are Buddhist, aren't they</u>?

A: Yes, that is true.

B: <u>The building is really magnificent.</u>

A: Sure. It is made up of several halls. Now let's walk into the forecourt through this gate. <u>On either side you can see a drum tower or a bell tower.</u>

B: Why are so many tourists standing in line before the bell tower?

A: They are waiting for their turns to strike the bell, <u>because they believe it will bring them good luck</u>. And bell-striking is one of the oldest Chinese traditions.

B: It seems the bell is made of bronze. <u>How long has it been hanging here</u>?

A: It is centuries old. Please look at the four figures in front of you.

B: <u>Oh, dear! What are these</u>? They frightened me.

A: They are four guardian warriors.

B: I see. <u>They stand there day and night guarding the hall.</u>

A: Exactly. Well, we are now in the Grand Hall. <u>Look up at the giant golden Buddha.</u> It is always smiling.

B: Yeah, who is it?

A: It's Maitreya Buddha, also called the laughing monk.

Appendix 2 Listening material

Listening II

Visiting Leshan Giant Buddha of Sichuan

A: Ladies and gentlemen, we've arrived at the tourist site of Leshan Giant Buddha. Please take your valuables with you and get off one by one.

B: What a magnificent Buddha! From this angle I could hardly see his head. The Buddha looks like a hill.

A: Yes, it is. The Giant Buddha is 71 meters high. There goes a saying, "The hill is a Buddha and the Buddha is a hill." It is the biggest Maitreya Buddha in the world.

B: It's an amazing stone statue. How was it chiseled（凿出） out of the mountain?

A: It was very hard to chisel Leshan Giant Buddha from the mountain. It was recorded that it took 90 years for the people of 4 dynasties to complete the huge project.

B: Look, what are those on the Buddha's head? They look like stone balls.

A: They are hair curls of the Giant Buddha. Each of them is as large as a round table.

B: Amazing! Look at his ears. They are so big.

A: Right. Each of his ears is seven meters long. Two men can hide inside each of them. Look down at his feet. Over 100 men can sit down on each of its 8.5-meter- wide insteps.

B: Fantastic! Leshan Giant Buddha is really giant. It's a marvel of the stone sculptures in the world.

A: Now we have reached the feet of the Giant Buddha. Look up at the Buddha!

B: Oh, we are all dwarfs（矮子） compared with the Buddha.

A: Now you can take pictures in front of it. It's time for free sightseeing. Have fun!

B: Thanks!

Item 10 Tours of Historical Sites

Model 1: A Tour of the Forbidden City

TASK4 Listen and Answer

1. What is the other name of the Palace Museum?
2. Who lived in the Forbidden City?
3. What was the Hall of Supreme Harmony used for?
4. Where did the feudal emperors handle their daily affairs?
5. When was the Hall of Preserving Harmony built?

Model 2: The Tour of the Great Wall

TASK4 Listen and Answer

1. When did the construction of the Great wall start?

2. How long is the Great Wall?
3. What are the towers on the wall?
4. Why did the ancient people build the Great Wall?
5. What's the meaning of "guan"?

Model 3: The Tianyi Pavilion Library

TASK3 Listen and Answer

1. Where is the Tianyi Pavilion located?
2. Who is the host of the Tianyi Pavilion?
3. What are the strict family rules of the Tianyi Pavilion?
4. What are the rich sources of the books in the Tianyi Pavilion?
5. What is the unique architecture of the Tianyi Pavilion?

TASK5 More Oral and Listening Practice:

Listening I

Visiting Mogao Grottos

T: My goodness, the Mogao Grottos have five stories.

G: <u>They are more than 1,600 meters long from north to south</u>.

T: Amazing! Some stand alone, and others are together. All are arranged in <u>perfect order</u>.

G: In the Yungang Grottos and the Longmen Grottos, statues are carved out of rock, but here they are sculpted out of clay.

T: <u>How did they make it</u>?

G: A local plant from the desert here was used to wrap the <u>wooden skeleton</u>, and then clay was used for sculpture.

T: <u>But they don't look like they are sculpted with clay</u>.

G: Because the statues were painted. It's called painted sculpture.

T: Those <u>ancient craftsmen</u> were really smart.

G: There is a <u>big collection</u> of murals in the Mogao Grottos, too. People believe there may be as many as 45,000 <u>square meters</u> of them. If they were put end to end, they would <u>form</u> a two-meter-high, 25-kilometer-long art gallery.

T: Wow, that's <u>really wonderful</u>.

Listening II

Lao She Teahouse

Lao She Teahouse, established in <u>1988</u>, is named for the <u>famous Chinese author</u>, Lao She, and one of his better-known works, "Teahouse". At the teahouse, customers sit in <u>an old Beijing setting</u>, drink the best teas in China, watch all kinds of <u>traditional Chinese performance art</u>, and enjoy delicious traditional Beijing <u>delicacies</u> which were eaten by Qing

Dynasty emperors. Since its opening, Lao She Teahouse has <u>entertained</u> many famous people from China and all over the world; <u>as a result</u>, the Teahouse is well-known in <u>many different countries</u>. In 1994, former United States President, George Bush visited the teahouse. Other <u>personages</u> include former <u>United Nations General Secretary</u> Kurt Waldheim and the Singaporean President, Wang Dingchang.

Item 11   Tour of Chinese Characteristic Culture

Model 1: Tai Chi

TASK4 Listen and Answer

1. What does Tai Chi mean?
2. What's the feature of Tai Chi, compared with other martial arts?
3. What's the benefit of playing Tai Chi?
4. What are the essentials for playing Tai Chi?
5. Is Tai Chi easy to learn?

Model 2: Spring Festival

TASK4 Listen and Answer

1. What's the relationship between Helen and Mr. Bush?
2. Why do Chinese people like firecrackers? What does it mean?
3. Where did Mr. Bush have his Nianyefan?
4. What about Chinese cuisine? Does Mr. Bush like it?
5. What else did Mr. Bush do after the feast?

Model 3: Peking Opera

TASK4 Listen and Answer

1. What are they going to do this Sunday evening?
2. What is Peking Opera?
3. Is Peking Opera popular in China? Why?
4. How many character types in Peking Opera? What are they?
5. What are actors and actresses in Peking Opera famous for?

Model 4: China–Home of Tea

TASK3 Listen and Answer

1. What are well-known for more than a thousand years and have been important Chinese exports?
2. It is said that China is the home of tea. Do you agree? Why?
3. How many types of Chinese tea are there?
4. Why do we say tea-drinking is an art in China?

5. What do scenic areas do in order to let tourists have a better understanding of Chinese tea and tea culture?

TASK5 More Oral and Listening Practice
Listening I

Traditional Chinese Festivals

A: Tomorrow is a <u>traditional</u> Chinese festival, the Dragon Boat Festival. <u>Would you like to go to</u> my hometown to eat Zongzi?

B: Great, thank you! Do you <u>have a holiday on</u> the Dragon Boat Festival?

A: Yes, we have holidays on festivals such as the <u>Spring Festival</u>, <u>Labor Day</u>, the Dragon Boat Festival and <u>National Day</u>.

B: Are the holidays long? How many days?

A: The statutory holidays for the Spring Festival and National Day are 3 days, while those for Labor Day and the Dragon Boat Festival are 1 day. My family <u>travels to South China</u> during this year's Spring Festival.

B: Spring Festival is <u>the biggest festival</u> in China, isn't it?

A: Yes, it is. It's <u>as lively as Christmas Day</u> in your country.

B: What other traditional festivals does China have?

A: There are Lantern Festival, Mid-autumn Festival, Qingming Festival and so on.

B: <u>What special food</u> do you have at the festivals?

A: We have, for example, Jiaozi, Yuanxiao, and mooncake.

Listening II

Going to a Dragon Dance

A: Hello, Mr. Brown, <u>this is Lan speaking</u>.

B: Yes?

A: Would you please tell your <u>group members</u> that tonight we are going to enjoy a Dragon Dance at Tianyi Square?63

B: A Dragon Dance?

A: Have you ever heard of it?

B: Yes, but I think it must be scary to see a monster <u>dancing at night</u>.

A: Oh, you're quite <u>mistaken</u>. China's legendary dragon is not the monster encountered in Western mythology, but a benign creature symbolizing <u>good fortune</u>.

B: Really?

A: Yes. In ancient times, dragon <u>were believed to</u> bring rain in times of drought, <u>keep away</u> misfortune, and bring good luck to all who need his help. This is why the dragon dance has become the most popular form of <u>entertainment</u> at the <u>folk</u> festivals, especially during <u>the Spring Festival</u>.

B: It must have a long history then.

A: You're right. The custom can be <u>traced back</u> at least to the Han Dynasty some <u>2,000</u> years ago. Usually, five to nine dragons danced together because in China the numbers five and nine <u>stand for good luck</u> and nobility.

B: OK. Miss Lan, I will tell everyone in the group not to miss it. <u>Thank you for arranging it</u>.

A: <u>That's my pleasure</u>. See you at 7:00 p.m. then.

B: See you.

Item 12 Shopping

Model 1: Chinese Calligraphy

  TASK4 Listen and Answer

  1. Where are they going to buy Chinese Calligraphy?
  2. What are the so-called "four treasures of the study"?
  3. What is the function of the "four treasures of the study"?
  4. What is the reappearance of this historic innovative process?
  5. Where is their car now?

Model 2: Antiques and Ancient Furniture

  TASK4 Listen and Answer

  1. What did the shop assistant first introduce to them?
  2. What's the main kind of traditional Chinese paintings?
  3. Why did the customer like the painting best?
  4. Why did the shop assistant say the customer was a good bargainer?
  5. How will the customer send the painting back to his country?

Model 3: Shopping Service

  TASK4 Listen and Answer

  1. What can you buy on this commercial street?
  2. What are the various commodities with distinguished culture?
  3. What are the numerous precious medicinal materials?
  4. What are the regulations on the purchase of Chinese medicinal materials?
  5. What are the regulations on the purchase of antiques?

Model 4: Jade Culture

  TASK3 Listen and Answer

  1. When did the Chinese begin to use jade?
  2. Where was Yangshao culture mainly located?
  3. Why was jade used in tombs?

4. Why can gold, silver, and bronze not exceed the spiritual position that jade has acquired in peoples' minds?

5. What happened to the jade in Shang and Zhou dynasties?

TASK5 More Oral and Listening Practice:
Listening I

At the Jewelry's Store.

A: Can I help you, madam?

B: Yes, I'd like <u>to buy some presents</u> for my friends.

A: Would you like jewelry? Today is <u>Mother's Day</u> and all the jewelry is on sale at Rich's store.

B: That's great. <u>Do you have gold</u> jewels?

A: Yes, we have 24K and <u>18K</u> gold necklaces, chains, and earrings.

B: May I have a look?

A: Sure. <u>Here is a nice gold necklace</u>. Its regular price is <u>$56</u>, and now you can have it with a twenty percent discount.

B: It's very elegant. <u>I'll take it</u>.

A: All right. Is there anything else you want?

B: Will you show me that <u>key ring</u>?

A: Yes, here you are.

Listening II

At the Shop

A: Good morning, sir. May I help you?

B: Yes, can you <u>suggest a gift for a 12-year-old girl</u>?

A: How about some dolls? Girls at that age are especially <u>fond of them</u>.

B: She has already got plenty of dolls. I'd like to <u>give her something different</u> this time.

A: Maybe you can buy her a watch. You see, I have a <u>very wide selection</u> of watches.

B: This is a good idea. Can you <u>recommend one</u> for me?

A: This kind of watch is <u>the latest fashion</u>. It's very popular among children. Furthermore, the <u>quality is excellent</u> and it is cheap, too.

B: I suppose my daughter will like it. <u>What do you charge for it</u>?

A: 25 dollars.

B: Well, could you wrap it up for me?

A: Certainly. I'm sure your daughter <u>will like this beautiful</u> watch.

B: Thank you.

A: You're welcome.

Appendix 2 Listening material

Item 13 Handling Problems & Emergencies

Model 1: A Delayed Flight

TASK4 Listen and Answer
1. When did the flight plan to arrive?
2. Why was the flight delayed?
3. About how long will the tourist wait?
4. What's the guide's suggestion?
5. Did the tourist accept his idea?

Model 2: Calling the First Aid Center

TASK4 Listen and Answer
1. What happened to the patient?
2. What will happen if the patient isn't treated in time?
3. Where did they carry him into?
4. When will the patient recover?
5. Who will take care of him?

Model 3: First Aid Techniques

TASK3 Listen and Answer
1. What causes sudden heart attack?
2. What's the main figure of the artificial respiration?
3. What should be done first for the artificial respiration?
4. Which fingers do you use to do the job?
5. About how long will the action take for each time?

TASK5 More Oral and Listening Practice:
Listening I

The Delayed Flight

A: Hello, I have a ticket for the 8:00 flight to Guangzhou.
B: I'm so sorry that the flight has been delayed due to <u>the inclement weather</u>.
A: When will the plane be ready for take-off?
B: Well, it could be as soon as within <u>a few hours</u>, or as late as tomorrow morning. We're so sorry to <u>trouble you</u>. And we'd like to offer you a room <u>for free</u> at the hotel.
A: Where's the hotel? Is it far from here?
B: No. It's just <u>down the road</u>.
A: Will you contact us as soon as the plane is ready?

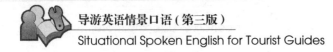

B: Of course. We'll send a shuttle van to pick you up.

A: Thank you very much.

Listening II

About the Toilet

A: Maintenance Department. Can I help you?

B: Yes, there seems to be something wrong with the toilet.

A: We'll send someone to repair it immediately. What's your room number, please?

B: 1287.

A: May I come in?

B: Come in.

A: The toilet doesn't flush.

B: Let me see. Oh, it's clogged... It's all right now. You may try it.

A: Yes, it's working now. Thank you.

B: You're welcome. Anything else?

A: The water tap drips all night long. I can hardly sleep.

B: I'm very sorry, sir. Some part needs to be replaced. I will be back soon.

Item 14 Handling Customer Complaints

Model 1: Complaining about the Food

TASK4 Listen and Answer

1. Why did the tourist say that the food there is so terrible?

2. What will the guide do for the guest?

3. When will they serve the changed food?

4. Will they make any discount? How much?

5. What's the tourist's reaction to the result?

Model 2: A Tour Guide or a Shopping Guide

TASK4 Listen and Answer

1. What happened to today's tour guide according to the tourist?

2. What led to the situation?

3. What about the other reason?

4. What's the tour escort's opinion on this reason?

5. What's the responsibility of a tour guide according to the tour escort in the text?

Model 3: A Complaint Letter on Holiday Booking

TASK3 Listen and Answer

1. What does the writer complain about?

2. When did the writer book the room?

3. What happened to the writer when she arrived at the hotel?
4. What happened to the writer then?
5. How long did the writer stay in the other hotel?

TASK5 More Oral and Listening Practice

Listening I

Complaining about the Facilities in the Hotel Room

A: I cannot suffer any more!

B: What happened?

A: The facilities in my room are so poor! The air conditioning broke down when I just turned it on.

B: In that case, you could call maintenance.

A: Look, that's the serious problem! I have asked the maintenance department several times, but no one responded.

B: Unbelievable! They should be at their place for 24 hours. What happened?

A: At last, I called the reception desk. And they told me that all their repairmen are busy now.

B: What?! All of them?

A: Yes, the receptionist said so.

B: What's wrong with them? I will call the manager to ask for an explanation.

A: OK, thank you.

B: You are welcome.

Listening II

Complaining about Room Cleaning

A: Good afternoon. May I help you?

B: Good afternoon. Why has my room not been cleaned so far?

A: I am sorry. We'll solve this problem as soon as possible.

B: And it's so annoying that when I asked for an extra bag for dry cleaning and I was told they are unavailable.

A: Thank you for pointing out this problem. I will investigate right away.

B: Besides, when I asked for a little more variety of fruits, I was told most of the fruits were out of season.

A: I'll report to the manager that you have not experienced our usual good service.

B: Furthermore, the room attendant always shuts the door hard when she finishes the turn-down service.

A: I do apologize that you have been troubled. I assure you the problems won't happen again. We are sorry again.

Item 15 Checking Out

Model 1: Checking Out

TASK4 Listen and Answer

1. Who wants to check out?
2. What's the room number?
3. How many nights have the guests stayed in the hotel?
4. When did the group arrive at the hotel?
5. Does the hotel accept credit cards?

Model 2: Paying by Credit Card

TASK4 Listen and Answer

1. Who wants to check out? What's his name and room number?
2. How many nights has the guest stayed in the hotel?
3. How did the guest pay for his breakfast?
4. What is the guest folio?
5. What does the clerk do with the guest's credit card?

Model 3: Paying with a Traveler's Check

TASK4 Listen and Answer

1. Who wants to check out? What's his name and room number?
2. What charges does the bill include?
3. How does the guest pay for his bill?
4. What does the clerk ask the guest to do when using the traveler's check?
5. What does the clerk give to the guest after settling the payment?

Model 4: Checkout Service Procedures

TASK3 Listen and Answer

1. What does the clerk ask the guest to show before checking out?
2. What should the clerk do before printing out the bill?
3. What should the clerk do after printing out the bill?
4. What should the clerk do after the guest checks the bill?
5. What should the clerk say to the guest after finishing checking out?

TASK5 More Oral and Listening Practice
Listening I

Exchanging Money

Cashier: Good afternoon! Can I help you?
Guest: Yes, I need to <u>change some money</u>.

Cashier:	What would you like?
Guest:	What is the rate of exchange for the Euro?
Cashier:	It's 1:7 to the Euro at the moment.
Guest:	Well, I would like to change 500 Euros this time.
Cashier:	Good. Can I have your passport for a moment?
Guest:	Yes. Here you are.
Cashier:	Thank you. 500 Euros will be 3,500 yuan. Please fill in this exchange memo and sign your name on it.
Guest:	I'll take care of it. ... Is that all right?
Cashier:	Yes, here is the change and your invoice. Keep this exchange memo.
Guest:	Thank you for your help. Goodbye.
Cashier:	Goodbye, Mr. Clarke. We hope you'll have a good journey.

Listening II

A Mistake on the Hotel Bill

Staff:	Can I help the next person in line, please?
Guest:	I'd like to check out, please.
Staff:	Your room number, please?
Guest:	Room 1408.
Staff:	One moment while I print out your bill.
Guest:	Hmm, I thought the rate was 480 per night.
Staff:	Exactly, sir.
Guest:	What's this charge of RMB 160?
Staff:	Oh, that's a 10 percent service charge.
Guest:	Oh, OK. And this shows that I have a 108 minibar bill. But I didn't use it.
Staff:	Oh, I'm terribly sorry. This must be a mistake. I'll correct it for you right away. Do you want to put your charges on your AMEX card?
Guest:	Yes. That's right.
Staff:	Let me take an imprint of it, please.
Guest:	Here you are.
Staff:	OK. Here's your copy, Mr. Smith. I hope you've enjoyed your stay with us.

Item 16 Farewell, China

Model 1: See you Again Soon

TASK4 Listen and Answer

1. What should a tour guide do before the tour group leaves the hotel?

2. What does the tour guide do after the guests get on the coach?

3. How does the tour guide say goodbye to the guest?

4. What does the old Chinese saying "Even a good banquet has an end" mean?

5. How does the tour leader say thank you to the tour guide for her considerate service?

Model 2: Seeing Guests off at the airport

TASK4 Listen and Answer

1. What does the tour guide do to help the tour group check in at the airport?

2. What does the tour guide give to the guests?

3. Where do the guests go then?

4. What should the guests take with them when checking in?

5. How do the tour guide and the guests say goodbye to each other?

Model 3: A Farewell Speech

TASK3 Listen and Answer

1. Where does the tour guide come from?

2. Which scenic spots have they visited?

3. Which food have they tasted?

4. Try to explain the Chinese saying "there is nothing more delightful than to meet friends from afar" in English.

5. What information shall a farewell speech include?

TASK5 More Oral and Listening Practice
Listening I

Check-in at the Train Station

A: Shall we check in now?

B: Yes, let's go on board to avoid the last-minute rush.

A: Please put your baggage on the counter for security inspection.
OK. Let's move on to the ticket control.

B: Where is the ticket control for going to Hangzhou?

A: Over there, at Gate 3. Please have the tickets ready and wait to get them punched.

B: To which platform are we going?

A: Platform 3. Let me help you with the suitcase.

B: Thank you.

A: Here we are. Platform 3. The car is just ahead. Car 6. Please get on.

B: It's a nice car. My seat is there.

A: Where would you like me to put the suitcase, on the rack or under the seat?

B: On the rack, please. Thank you.

A: Good. Is there anything else I can do for you?

B: No, thank you. You have been a great help. Thank you, indeed.

A: It's my pleasure. The train starts in a few minutes. Now it's time for us to say goodbye. I wish you a happy journey and a pleasant stay in Hangzhou.

B: Goodbye, Mr. Guide. Thank you for your help.

Listening II

Seeing Guests Off

G: Is everything in order now?

T1: Yes. When will the plane take off?

G: At eleven thirty. There is still half an hour to go. Please take care of your luggage.

T2: Mr.Hu, during our trip in the past ten days, you've shown your concern for us in every respect. I really don't know how to express my gratitude.

G: Thank you for saying so.

T1: Before I came here, I only had an understanding of China from books, papers, television and films. Now I've seen China with my own eyes.

G: If you have another chance, come to China again.

T1: It's a pity we haven't had enough time for many other places.

G: Welcome to China again. You're always welcome.

T1: Wonderful. I hope we'll keep in touch.

G: It's time to board the plane.

T2: Goodbye, Mr.Hu. Thank you very much.

G: Goodbye. Bon voyage!

References
参考文献

1. 关肇远. 导游英语口语 [M]. 2版. 北京：高等教育出版社，2009.
2. 徐辉. 出境旅游领队实务（双语）[M]. 北京：中国财政经济出版社，2016.
3. 纪春，裴松青. 英语导游教程 [M]. 2版. 北京：旅游教育出版社，2008.
4. 冯玮. 新编导游英语 [M]. 2版. 武汉：武汉大学出版社，2007.
5. 梅德明. 高级口译教程 [M]. 2版. 上海：上海外语教育出版社，2000.
6. 朱华. 旅游英语教程 [M]. 2版. 北京：高等教育出版社，2011.
7. 魏国富. 实用旅游英语口语 [M]. 上海：复旦大学出版社，2003.
8. 郭兆康. 饭店情景英语 [M]. 上海：复旦大学出版社，2016.
9. 谢先泽. 中国旅游：英语读本 [M]. 成都：西南财经大学出版社，2006.
10. 初丽岩. 旅游交际英语通 [M]. 4版. 上海：华东师范大学出版社，2020.
11. 毕洪英. 敢说导游服务英语 [M]. 北京：机械工业出版社，2004.
12. 苏静，范作为. 导游英语 [M]. 2版. 北京：化学工业出版社，2013.
13. 吴云，钱嘉颖. 旅游实践英语：下册 [M]. 3版. 北京：旅游教育出版社，2021.
14. 袁智敏. 旅游英语 [M]. 2版. 北京：北京大学出版社，2013.
15. 赵伐，胡兰. 旅游英语 [M]. 2版. 杭州：浙江大学出版社，2013.
16. 赵宝国，谭晓蓉. 21世纪实用旅游英语教程 [M]. 上海：学林出版社，2005.
17. 孙小珂. 新编饭店英语 [M]. 修订版. 武汉：武汉大学出版社，2007.
18. 李燕，徐静. 旅游英语 [M]. 3版. 北京：清华大学出版社，2017.
19. 南凡，刘素花. 旅游英语 [M]. 2版. 北京：高等教育出版社，2011.
20. 杨华. 实用旅游英语 [M]. 2版. 北京：中国人民大学出版社，2012.
21. 张靖. 英语导游基础教程 [M]. 北京：清华大学出版社，2009.
22. 王浪. 中国著名旅游景区导游词精选（英汉对照）[M]. 北京：旅游教育出版社，2010.
23. 张建融，杨志超. 杭州英语导游 [M]. 北京：中国旅游出版社，2013.
24. 段开成，吕迎春，黄宝琴. 导游英语听与说 [M]. 天津：南开大学出版社，2001.
25. 吴云，邵华. 21世纪实用饭店情景英语教程 [M]. 上海：学林出版社，2005.
26. 蒋磊. 旅游英语综合教程 [M]. 北京：外语教学与研究出版社，2018.
27. 杨志忠，杨义德，许艾君. 涉外导游英语 [M]. 上海：复旦大学出版社，2007.